DAVIS ALLEN

DAVIS ALLEN

FORTY YEARS OF **INTERIOR DESIGN**
AT SKIDMORE, OWINGS & MERRILL

MAEVE SLAVIN

RIZZOLI
NEW YORK

For James Slavin, Architect

First published in the United States of America by
Rizzoli International Publications, Inc.
300 Park Avenue South, New York, NY 10010

Library of Congress Cataloging-in-Publication Data

Slavin, Maeve.
    Davis Allen : 40 years of interior design at Skidmore, Owings &
Merrill / Maeve Slavin.
        p. cm.
    Includes bibliographical references.
    ISBN 0-8478-1255-3
    1. Allen, Davis Brewster, 1916- —Criticism and interpretation.
2. Interior decoration—United States—History—20th century.
3. Skidmore, Owings & Merrill.   I. Allen, Davis Brewster, 1916–
II. Title.
NK2004.3.A45S5 1990   90-8456
729′.092—dc20   CIP

FRONT COVER: Executive reception area, Continental Grain
headquarters, New York City. Photography © Ezra Stoller/Esto
Photographics Inc.
BACK COVER: Andover chair designed by Davis Allen.

Designed by Charles Davey
Set in type by David E. Seham Associates, Metuchen, New Jersey
Printed and bound by Toppan Printing Company, Singapore

CONTENTS

PHOTOGRAPHY CREDITS

Numbers refer to pages

Davis Allen, 11, 12(right), Jaime Ardiles-Arce, 82–83, 85, 86–87, 92–93, 94–95, 127; Morley Baer, 33; Lee Boltin, 34, 37(bottom), 38(top); Thom Duncan © 1986, 18; Philip Ennis Photography, 128, 129(bottom); Alexandre Georges/Courtesy of Chase Manhattan Archives, 41, 43(bottom), 45; Carol Groh & Associates, 116(top), 118–119, 120–121, 122(bottom), 123, 124–125; Hedrich-Blessing, 26, 28(top), 31, 129(top); Hickory Business Furniture (HBF), 116(bottom); Bob Hollingsworth, 76(top); Jack Horner, 68(top), 84(left); Wolfgang Hoyt, 100, 103(bottom), 106, 108, 109(bottom), 111, 114, 117(left); Jan Jachniewicz/Courtesy of Chase Manhattan Archives, 42, 43(top), 44; Kaufmann & Fabry Co., 16(center); Knoll International, 14; Arthur Lavine/Courtesy of Chase Manhattan Archives, 40; Fred Lyon, 51(bottom), 58, 76(bottom), 77(top), 78–79, 80–81; Gregory Murphey, 97, 98(bottom); Cervin Robinson, 62; Durston Saylor, 130–131; Maeve Slavin, 15; Stendig International, 2, 115, 117(right top & bottom); Ezra Stoller © Esto Photographics, 13, 17, 19, 22–23, 24–25, 27, 28(bottom), 29, 30, 35, 36, 37(top), 38(bottom), 39, 46–47, 48–49, 60–61, 63, 64–65, 66(bottom), 67, 68(bottom), 69, 70–71, 73, 74–75, 84(right), 89, 89, 90–91; Swishee, Chicago, 16(bottom); Tru/Color Photographers, 12(left); R. Wenkam, 51(top); Katherine Young, 16(top).

ACKNOWLEDGMENTS

Compiling the achievements of a distinguished forty-year career with accuracy and fairness can present a daunting challenge. However, my experience in the preparation of this book has happily confirmed Davis Allen's adage that "If you ask questions and tell people what you're doing, they are usually very helpful." The response to my requests for information and commentary was unhesitating, and my gratitude for generous cooperation is owed to more people than I have space to list here.

I benefited from the wisdom and humor of Davis Allen in many meetings and conversations. His habit, to which his colleagues attest in these pages, of teaching without preaching—of suggesting an idea that invariably leads to a better solution—was an education in itself.

The firm of Skidmore, Owings & Merrill, in particular the partners in the New York office, reacted with unreserved enthusiasm to my proposal to chronicle Allen's career. SOM provided the majority of the illustrative materials with open access to supporting information. Partners Donald Smith, Raul de Armas, and Michael McCarthy were especially helpful in assessing Allen's role in the development of the firm's interior design heritage. The assistance of Kathryn Hamilton, Director of Communications for SOM, was pivotal to my research. Aided by Betsey Feeley, she worked unstintingly to assemble the hundreds of photographs and documents required to obtain the permissions necessary for publication.

Vignettes of Allen, elicited during interviews with Gordon Bunshaft, Margo Grant, Carol Groh, and Charles Pfister, add considerably, I believe, to the depth of the study. These warm tributes were completely spontaneous and sincerely offered. I very much appreciate their gracious contributions.

My editor, Robert Janjigian, has been a paradigm of patience, forebearance, and professionalism. His encouragement gave this project its impetus and immediacy. My gratitude to him, to our art director, Charles Davey, and to Rizzoli International Publications is unbounded.

M.S.

PART ONE: THE EARLY YEARS, 1916–1950

Davis Allen joined Skidmore, Owings & Merrill (SOM) in 1950 as a junior architectural designer. He had hoped to find a secure job where he could expect to stay at least five years. He actually had found a home.

In the intervening forty years, and since 1965 with the rank of Associate Partner, Senior Interior Designer, Allen collaborated with three generations of SOM partners. Semiretired since 1985, he has continued to act as mentor, design critic, and trusted contributor to this multidisciplined architectural firm whose influence has been felt worldwide. Many of the designers he led in more than fifty blue-ribbon projects have gone on to make distinguished careers within SOM, at other firms, or under their own names. Three have received the coveted *Interiors* magazine Designer of the Year Award; several, including Allen himself, are members of the prestigious *Interior Design* magazine Hall of Fame.

At SOM, which has been called a university of postgraduate studies, Davis Allen is regarded as dean. In the profession he helped to establish—the total design of the interior corporate environment with furniture, art, and functional and decorative objects integrated into a comprehensively planned space—he is an institution. A scion of pioneer stock, Allen himself is a pioneer in the field of interior architecture, which became an acknowledged discipline only in the 1950s.

Allen traces his ancestry to the earliest European settlers in North America: some of his ancestors landed at Plymouth Rock; others made their way as fur traders up the Mississippi River to St. Louis. Never one to call attention to his lineage, Allen downplayed his Mayflower association, remarking that "What you realize about that time is that *everybody* was an immigrant and *everybody* was recent." Descendants of these pioneers pushed the envelope of the frontier outward; in the 1840s they reached the Great Plains, where Allen's great-grandfather founded a chain of banks in rural towns and his grandmother enlivened his childhood imagination with tales of the Indian wars. Allen's father, born in 1889, could recall his own meeting as a small boy with aged great-aunts, the Misses Flavia and Sabra Brewster,

who remembered waving to George Washington riding past their home on horseback "when we were about your age."

Allen thus carried with him a personal sense of the sweep of American history, although he would learn by firsthand experience how brief it was by comparison with the ancient cultures of Europe, Africa, and Asia. In a remark worthy of Gertrude Stein, he explained his sentiments: "It's a very short story. I don't forget it because I remember it." The energy of that still nascent history has enlivened Allen's work as a designer of interior space and of furniture produced by such bellwether industry names as Steelcase, GF, Stow & Davis, Stendig, Bernhardt, Hickory Business Furniture, and Jack Lenor Larsen.

Unlike those masters who seem to have been born with pencils grasped in infantile fingers, Davis Allen did not slide without hitch or hesitation into the study of architecture. His odyssey of self-discovery lasted until his early twenties. He told, with characteristic relish, of a family friend's query upon hearing that Allen had entered Yale: "Why is he studying architecture? I never saw him draw a thing in his life!" His timing was fortuitous, however. Davis Allen came to maturity as a designer at exactly the moment when corporate America began its quest for a new identity to express the sense of optimism and rebirth that accompanied the end of the Second World War.

Davis Brewster Allen was born on July 13, 1916, in Ames, Iowa, a descendant of Elder Brewster of the Massachusetts Bay Colony. One of five brothers, he grew up in the nearby town of Fort Dodge and later outside Chicago. Although the family had been rooted in the Middle West for three generations, his parents, Amiriah Lewis Allen and Esther Primrose Davis Allen, still spoke of New England and Europe with contagious nostalgia. At eighteen, Allen enrolled at Brown University, where he hoped to find the cozy little New England community of family legend. Instead, to his disappointment, he discovered that Providence in 1934 was "an industrial city full of smoke." He left in his sophomore year. His father shipped him out to a family farm in western Illinois, where

he was put in charge of milking fifty cows (fortunately, with the aid of an electric milker), and then to a ranch in Montana. In the interim he looked at Stanford University, with an eye to enrolling there, but decided it was too far from the East Coast and the gateway to Europe that it represents. In an attempt to formulate a more practical career plan, Allen decided to learn about manufacturing. He started at the bottom, working in Chicago at the Illinois Tool Works, where he packed machine screws to be used in the automobile plants of Detroit.

Allen was twenty-three years old when, for reasons that he cannot recall, he made up his mind to travel abroad and while so doing to study architecture. War clouds were gathering over Europe, however, and in the summer of 1939 he realized that he could wait no longer to make his Grand Tour. Instead of France and England, "where I really wanted to go," he set off for Sweden, which he figured would not immediately become a war zone and where he had heard that "they were doing modern things." He was armed with an introduction to Anders Tengbom, a young architect who had worked at Holabird & Root in Chicago and whose father was himself a leading architect. Under this aegis, Allen enrolled at Stockholm's Kungliga Tekniska Högskolan, the National Swedish Institute for Building Research. "Anders Tengbom introduced me to another Swede and he introduced me to another; soon I had a circle of friends, all because of one person." Allen would repeat this pattern throughout his travels, leading to the development of a global network of contacts and resources.

That summer Allen ran into a group of American architecture students, including William Hartmann, who would later become an SOM partner, and went with them to Finland on tour of the works of Alvar Aalto. The group visited buildings, met Aalto and his wife Aino, saw their glass and furniture, and experienced their philosophy of total design. In Sweden, Allen had already been impressed by the integration of arts and crafts: architecture, furniture, painting, sculpture, ceramics, glasswork, and weaving functioning as essential parts of

a whole. In Finland, he found the same holistic attitude. "I got a very strong sense of these things being related," he remembered.

In 1940, with Norway and Denmark occupied and the war already involving most of Western Europe, Allen decided to return home. The effect of his epiphany of total design would be revealed in projects throughout his career, from Mauna Kea in Hawaii to Paris, Jidda, Kuwait, and the glass-walled towers of corporate America from New York and Chicago to Kansas City and Nashville.

The faculty at the Yale University School of Architecture, where Allen enrolled in the fall of 1940, was more eclectic than that at Harvard under Walter Gropius and Marcel Breuer, or at the Illinois Institute of Technology (IIT) under Mies van der Rohe. "When I arrived at Yale, they were still under the influence of the Beaux Arts tradition as well as excited about the new architecture. It was a very healthy education." His instructors included Oscar Nitzchke and a young postgraduate architect, George Dudley, who would later become secretary to the Board of Design for the United Nations Headquarters. Nitzchke had worked with Le Corbusier and the Perret brothers; his Paris circle had included the De Stijl group and Picasso, Léger, and Miró, as well as the American Alexander Calder. On his weekends away from New Haven, Nitzchke mingled in New York with the painters Jackson Pollock, Franz Kline, Willem de Kooning, and Arshile Gorky. As Davis Allen at SOM would later open the minds of young designers to the larger world of contemporary artists and craftworkers, so Oscar Nitzchke brought the legendary figures of the mid-century avant-garde to life for his Yale students, creating, George Dudley later wrote, "a sense of sharing in the turbulence at the cutting edge."

A different turbulence, three years' service in the Army, interrupted Allen's studies. In the summer of 1946, before returning to Yale, he worked as an intern at SOM. Assigned to the Cincinnati Terrace Plaza Hotel project, he was excited by the inclusion of works by Joan Miró, Saul Steinberg, and Alexander Calder in the interior planning. After a final year at

OPPOSITE LEFT: The second of five sons of Amiriah and Esther Allen, Davis Allen (back row, third from left) joined the extended family on the occasion of his parents' Golden Wedding Anniversary.

OPPOSITE RIGHT: Allen's study of Islamic symbols and decorative themes began during his two-year stay in Istanbul, Turkey, in the early 1950s, and continued to absorb his interest in the course of the years that followed. Here, at Granada, Spain, in the 1980s, he rests in front of a Moorish screen.

ABOVE: During his 1946 summer vacation, Allen, a student at the Yale University School of Architecture, worked as a summer intern at Skidmore, Owings & Merrill's New York office. The Terrace Plaza Hotel, Cincinnati, was being designed that summer and the young intern was impressed by the inclusion of original works of art in the planning concept. The inclusion of a mural by Joan Miró in the dining room was one example of the firm's belief in "total design" which Allen also advocated as a primary tenet of interior architecture.

Yale, he returned to New York at the age of thirty-one.

Allen looks to that year, 1947, as a watershed in the evolution of the United States:

> When I was a child, and really until after the war, the greater part of this country was composed of small, country towns, connected by two-lane roads, generally gravel or macadam. There was no system of highways or communications as we have now. Things we take for granted today such as television and airlines hardly existed, and even telephones were fairly unusual. It was pretty primitive. When you went for a drive in the countryside you were liable to get stuck in the mud, and you'd have to get a farmer to pull you out with his tractor. After the war, when they began to pave the entire country, all that changed.

Indeed, "after the war" opened a period of unprecedented prosperity that was to last for twenty years. Corporate America, led by entrepreneurs "born in this century, tested by war and disciplined by a hard and bitter peace" in the words of President John Kennedy's Inaugural Address a generation later, began a growth curve that spread across the seas. These institutions looked to architects to delineate a new image, expressing the confidence of economic stability allied to visionary progress in a manner that was functional yet supremely elegant, and, of course, modern.

The new architecture was the embodiment of this paradigm. Its acceptance by such influential clients as the Rockefellers and certain enlightened corporations signaled a break with traditional attitudes to the workplace. This architecture demanded an innovative approach to the interior corporate environment, which with the exception of examples of integrated design such as Frank Lloyd Wright's Johnson Wax Company Administration Building (1936) and the General Motors Technical Center by the father-and-son team Eliel

and Eero Saarinen (1946–1957) had largely been ignored by American architects.

Few realized this more intensely than Hans and Florence Knoll, who in 1946 married and formed Knoll Associates, a partnership dedicated to the design and manufacture of furniture in the Bauhaus idiom. Since modern furniture required a modern setting, Florence Knoll, an architect trained under Eliel Saarinen and Mies van der Rohe, established the Knoll Planning Unit, an ancillary design studio that provided interior architectural and planning services to Knoll's furniture clients. In the late 1940s, under Mrs. Knoll's direction, the Knoll Planning Unit became, in effect, a kind of laboratory for the design of interior spaces and task-related furniture appropriate in materials and scale to the aesthetic of the new buildings. In the course of this research, redefinition of the office environment began to emerge as a key goal of interior design.

Allen went to work at the Knoll Planning Unit "because I knew that they believed in the integration of the arts." Resources during what Florence Knoll has called "the early years, the lean years" were limited. Allen confirmed the degree to which ingenuity was required to achieve a finished product. "For example, a conference table was a slab of plywood with chromed gas-pipe legs screwed on to it. It was later, when the wartime shortage of materials began to ease up, that the Knolls developed their sophistication."

To Allen, the Knolls' passion for design was emblematic of this period in New York.

> There were people who wanted to build new buildings that they hadn't been able to build because of the war and the Depression before that. And there were a lot of kids who'd been educated at Harvard or Yale, or IIT under Mies, and they were full of good ideas. The museums all grew at that time and began to build new buildings: the Museum of Modern Art, the Guggenheim, and the Whitney all

moved from townhouses, and the Metropolitan began to expand. And you had the painting of the New York School. There was dedication to building and creating, and there were clients with vision.

During the late 1940s, munificent clients funded projects that blazed the trail to the modern office environment that is now accepted as the norm: well-lit and empathetically colored spaces planned for efficiency and productivity; embellished with art, decorative objects, and plants; and furnished with desks and chairs that conform to the human anatomy. Such spaces create a sense of comfort that has been shown to have a measurable effect on employee morale. Allen remembers that SOM in the 1950s became among the first major architectural/engineering firms to include interior design in its professional repertory: "We asked ourselves if doing this total job, interiors as well as building architecture, would affect the people who worked in this new environment. We found that it did, in the way they dressed and in their general attitude. They liked having modern art in the cafeterias, public spaces, and general offices. They liked having new furniture and clean windows." Who wouldn't? it might be asked. But back in those "lean years" the force of the revelation was astounding, although it gradually became axiomatic in sound business practice.

After leaving the Knoll Planning Unit, Allen worked for a short time in the office of Raymond Loewy. Coming to the conclusion that he preferred the more rational process and broader scope of architectural design to that of industrial design, he moved on to the architectural firm of Harrison & Abramovitz, where the United Nations Headquarters project was on the boards. Here he again encountered Oscar Nitzchke, George Dudley, and many other acquaintances from Yale. This project, built on land donated by John D. Rockefeller, Jr., blessed by Robert Moses, and designed by a committee of world-class architects chaired by Wallace K. Harrison, with the dominating persona of Le Corbusier tow-

ering over everyone, was to be a dazzling architectural testament to prosperity and peace among the community of nations. It evoked the idealism of the period and symbolized the dawning of a new era of enlightenment. In addition to some space-planning exercises, Allen left his permanent mark in the public entry hall of the General Assembly building with fraternal-twin pieces of furniture: generously scaled marble-topped reception desks, one doughnut-shaped and one rectilinear, clad with teak panels in an undulating vertical pattern reminiscent of the sinuous elegance of an Aalto screen or the ceiling of the Finnish master's Viipuri library.

"Then, I guess I wanted more pay and I think probably more stimulating work," Allen recalled. "I also thought I should find somewhere and remain for a while, at least five years." His thoughts turned to SOM and undoubtedly to the Lever House project, then in the final design stage. The first of the sleek, transparent towers that would transform New York's Park Avenue, it was the ultimate example of the "turbulence at the cutting edge." It would serve as the master model for succeeding generations of lightweight glass and metal buildings around the world utilizing the latest technologies, materials, and structural systems to achieve an elegant and contemporary form.

"I went to Gordon Bunshaft and said that I'd like to join the firm. He seemed reluctant I thought, so I told him that I was very eager to work there and that I'd work without pay for several months and if that didn't suit, I would leave. Gordon immediately said that working for nothing was out of the question and hired me. As it turned out, over the years I worked more closely with him on more projects than with any other SOM partner."

The constrast between the stocky and sometimes irascible Bunshaft and the tall, stately and ever-courteous Allen could hardly be more extreme. Yet their professional relationship, based on mutual respect, endured until Bunshaft's retirement in 1979. In retrospect, Bunshaft paid Allen the highest compliment: "There is no question that Dave Allen is the best there is. He has natural taste and the imagination

RIGHT: **Louis Skidmore (top) and Nathaniel Owings (center) founded the firm that still bears their names in 1936. In 1939 they were joined by the engineer John O. Merrill (bottom). The partnership was further cemented by the marriage of Skidmore to Owings's sister Eloise.**

OPPOSITE: **SOM's Lever House, completed in 1952, was the first modern high-rise to appear on Manhattan's Park Avenue. Greatly admired for its innovative design, it was to serve as the master model for lightweight glass and steel buildings around the world.**

to create some wonderful things and without much fuss." Allen, too, appreciated the absence of what both plainspoken men call "fuss":

> With Gordon, there was never any fuss; he was direct and he was clear to me. He communicated with almost hieroglyphic indications but I could understand them. I would first try to give him what he asked for and then try to expand and explain why I thought it should be this other way. There was always an honest response from him. There was always honesty. If he didn't like it he told you so. And a large part of the pleasure of working with Gordon was the opportunity to contribute to the interiors and planning of good buildings.

Bunshaft and Allen collaborated on many of the most memorable projects in the prestigious history of SOM. Clients included such powerful giants of international commerce and finance as the Rockefeller brothers, Aristotle Onassis, and Gianni and Umberto Agnelli, as well as former President Lyndon Johnson. As SOM expanded, Davis Allen's talent, his ability to inspire his team by his unceasing search for excellence, his attention to detail, and his remarkable rapport with clients became a firm-wide resource. Beginning in the mid-1950s, Allen consulted on the interior design component of projects originating in the Chicago and San Francisco offices as well as in New York. As Bunshaft was to phrase it, "Dave Allen can do anything, and always with good taste. He has a natural talent and he grew with the office, as we all did."

Skidmore, Owings & Merrill was founded in 1936 by the architect brothers-in-law Louis Skidmore and Nathaniel Owings. Three years later the engineer John Merrill joined the triumvirate that continues to bear their names. In his memoir, *The Spaces in Between—An Architect's Journey,* Ow-

ings related his and Skidmore's pledge "to offer a multidisciplined service competent to design and build the multiplicity of shelters needed for man's habitat. We would build only in the vernacular of our own age. We felt we knew how to build a modern 'Gothic Builders Guild' practice and to apply the synergism of power thus created." The fledgling firm would combine group practice, good design, social change, and what Owings called "showmanship"; the ebullient Owings and the more saturnine Skidmore excelled no less in the latter than in their ability to create appropriate design solutions incorporating the vernacular of their age.

By 1950, the firm had seven partners, including Gordon Bunshaft, who was gradually assuming the design leadership of the New York office and had a staff of some forty design professionals. Their credentials included a range of housing, hospitality, and industrial projects for public- and private-sector clients. Lever House was to propel SOM into the business of corporate architecture in which the firm would become a preeminent exponent of the architectural language enunciated by Le Corbusier and Mies van der Rohe. Unlike these two giants of modernism whose personal signatures were writ large on their buildings, however, SOM continued the custom of group practice embodied in the founders' manifesto. "We always worked in teams," Allen said. "The teams were pyramid-shaped, with an administrative partner and a design partner at the top, then project managers, and then the teams organized in the various disciplines. On most jobs, I was in charge of the interior design team. And young designers obviously contributed to the design. That was part of how they got their training." Gordon Bunshaft expressed the result of team interaction in brusquer terms: "When you get down to it, you can make all sorts of claims about who did what. It becomes like a joint venture, each one respecting the other." In this collaborative milieu, Allen's reticent personality and unassuming manner found a home. The firm's faith in total design was also attractive. "We all worked together from the beginning of projects, so that the interior design team could make suggestions to the architects about the materials and the architectural elements of the interior space." Furniture, not available commercially in the abundance that was to emerge in the 1970s, was designed as needed: staircases and elevator cabs were created, finishes were specified, and details from bathroom fixtures to tableware were attended to.

Soon after Allen joined the firm, SOM received the commission to design a new branch of the Manufacturers Hanover Trust Bank (then Manufacturers Trust Company) on the corner of Fifth Avenue and Forty-third Street in New York. Louis Skidmore organized an in-house competition for the design. The winner was Charles Evans Hughes III, who received the prize of $35 and credit for proposing a concept that changed the basis of banking hall design from ornate, bulky masses to the pristine lightness of the glass box. Allen won the second prize of $25. SOM had not yet established an interior design department: the interiors of Lever House had been designed by Raymond Loewy, and the contract for this interior, based on SOM's concept, was awarded to the firm of Eleanor LeMaire. In slightly apologetic exculpation for the omission of a discipline that was to become one of the hallmarks of the firm's reputation, Bunshaft later offered a gruff explanation that summed up the attitude of the period: "After all, we were architects."

Allen was involved with one final detail of the bank project. "Gordon asked me to look at the plan for the penthouse executive suite. He said, 'I think the president needs a private bathroom. See how you can fit it in.'" Allen studied the plan and replied, "'I think he needs more than that. He needs a good plan.' So, I tidied it up." The project "came out pretty much as I suggested, including wide floor-to-ceiling doors with minimal hardware." Allen was then assigned to work as a junior architectural designer on the Istanbul Hilton Hotel, which SOM was designing in collaboration with Turkish architect Sedat Hakki Eldem. The drawings had to be completed in Istanbul in order to conform to Turkish building codes and standards, so "I was sent over there to represent the office in that process and in the construction phase."

Allen thus embarked on the first of a series of journeys that would take him around the world three times. His "post-graduate" education at SOM can be said to have been completed during this process of exposure to the culture and vernacular of the Middle East. Allen's immersion in its richness and the diversity of its historical references would be reflected in his later work in Hawaii, Saudi Arabia, and Kuwait, as well as in the distinctly more temperate climate of the North American corporate headquarters, where in determining the parameters of interior architecture and its embellishment Allen helped to define the corporate image as well.

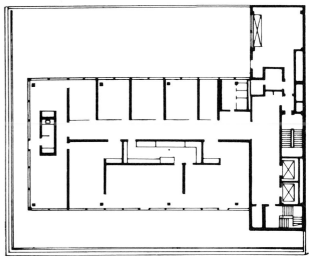

PART TWO: THE PROJECTS, 1950–1990

ISTANBUL HILTON HOTEL,
ISTANBUL, TURKEY, COMPLETED **1955**

PARTNER-IN-CHARGE: WILLIAM S. BROWN
DESIGN PARTNER: GORDON BUNSHAFT

Nat Owings has described the 300-room Istanbul Hilton Hotel as "an Arabian Nights job" in a "magic city." The commission came to the New York office in 1951, in association with the Turkish firm of Sedat Eldem. It was "a salubrious blend of strong Turkish architectural motifs and American plumbing and heating," Owings wrote. Sited overlooking the Bosporus strait that separates Asia and Europe, the building showed the disciplined hand and modern proclivities of Gordon Bunshaft in its meticulously engineered reinforced-concrete construction and rigid rectilinear form behind a façade of balconied recesses. The interiors, by contrast, reflect the influence of Professor Eldem in their "rich, lush, romantic Turkish" materials, colors, and forms.

Davis Allen is very clear about the extent of his responsibilities and involvement in every job throughout his career. Given his later mastery of interior design, a myth has grown up about his contribution to the Istanbul Hilton project. In his words:

> I started out working on the project in New York as a junior architectural designer. We worked with Sedat Eldem over here. The drawings were completed in Turkey, and I was sent along to Istanbul in the spring of 1953 to attend to unfinished design business. I stayed for two years without coming home to America. Now everyone believes that I did the interiors, which was not the case at all. It was hard to explain to the people in New York that I was designing landscaping, swimming pools, even Turkish towels and tiles.

Specifically, Allen helped to select materials for the tiled dome of the supper club structure, for mosaics in the public spaces, and for the concrete- and glass-inlaid mullioned windscreen of the cocktail and breakfast terrace. Beyond that, Allen assisted the local architects in the general outfitting of the building.

Allen's experience, however, went far beyond the practical exposure to construction-site techniques. First, it allowed the young architect a two-year immersion in a foreign capital city, with its layered associations to Roman, Byzantine, Ottoman, and Western influences. Allen learned "to use my eyes, and I guess my ears." Friends introduced by Professor Eldem and others gave him a knowledge of Middle Eastern culture that would serve him and SOM into the 1990s.

The second advantage was the proximity of Istanbul to Iran, Greece, Egypt, Lebanon, Syria, and Cyprus, all of which Allen visited, often with introductions. He was given entrée to important private houses, and his tutored memory to this day retains impressions of luxurious interiors, elegant furniture, splendid art and artifacts, the play of light within shaded rooms, and the sound of water falling from fountains and cascaded pools.

ABOVE: The Istanbul Hilton Hotel stands on a promontory overlooking the Bosporus strait.

OPPOSITE TOP: A typical guest floor seen in plan. The relationship between the structures of the hotel complex is shown in the section drawing.

OPPOSITE: Allen worked with the Turkish architects on the design and selection of decorative materials, including this tiled wall separating the hotel's main lobby from the writing room.

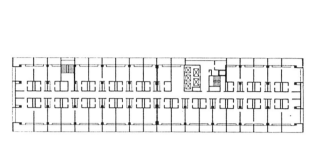

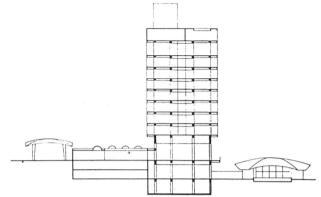

LEFT: The hotel's swimming pool area was designed by Allen, who also selected the tiles on the freestanding dining pavilion's roof.

BELOW: Allen composed a pattern based on traditional Turkish themes for the glass-and-metal windscreen of the cocktail terrace.

OPPOSITE: The interior furnishings in the main reception lobby reflect the Eastern and Western influences that distinguish the hotel's design. Traditional Turkish motifs on the tiled mosaic wall play against modern European furniture and architectural elements.

INLAND STEEL COMPANY,
CHICAGO, ILLINOIS, COMPLETED **1958**

PARTNER-IN-CHARGE: WILLIAM HARTMANN
DESIGN PARTNER: BRUCE J. GRAHAM

Davis Allen's two years in Istanbul opened an unexpected door for his reentry to professional life in America. As design of the Inland Steel Company headquarters was under discussion in the Chicago office of SOM, Inland's president, Leigh Block, and his wife, Mary, paid a visit to Istanbul. The Hilton was in its final stage when the SOM partners asked Allen to look after these clients. "I introduced them to my Turkish, English, and Egyptian friends. I remember we went to lunch at the British Embassy and had a ride on the ambassador's yacht. We got along very well, and I guess when they went home they asked Gordon Bunshaft to lend me to the Chicago office to work on their project."

Allen believed for some time that he had been banished to Chicago as punishment for some unfathomed infraction. "It was a mystery to me why, after I'd been back in New York for about ten minutes, I was sent right out to Chicago. It wasn't until much later that I found out the reason, when Leigh Block casually mentioned that he and Mary had personally requested it."

Inland Steel was to occupy the top eight floors of the nineteen-story structure, the first major new building the Loop had seen in more than twenty years. "It was," Allen recalled, "quite something for Chicago in those days."

Mrs. Block, the daughter of Albert Lasker, a Chicago advertising tycoon, had inherited a strong interest in modern painting; the Blocks owned an enviable collection that included works by Rousseau, Van Gogh, and Bonnard. The new headquarters was to be embellished with examples of contemporary American masterworks that would be specially commissioned and purchased. Art was integrated into the interior in the planning phase of the project, dictating a rather reserved background palette of grays, tans, and blacks. The Blocks requested that steel be used in the furniture and finishings: they wanted the interior to reflect modern design to underscore the material that was their stock-in-trade. Allen succinctly recapitulated the most significant parameter: "They didn't want any of that pseudo-Chippendale baloney."

Allen was given carte blanche to design the general office floors, executive offices, boardroom, lobby, private dining rooms, and cafeteria. The resources of Steelcase and Stow & Davis were called into play to manufacture designs that were revolutionary at the time. Allen's first chair was an executive lounge with leather seats and industrial steel-mesh frames on black matte steel legs, custom fabricated by Edgewater, a small New York workshop. The boardroom table, shaped like a surfboard, was manufactured by Stow & Davis with a laminated walnut top on double pedestals of polished stainless steel. Boardroom chairs were leather upholstered on splayed, slender legs by Steelcase. In contrast to the linoleum-topped gray "monsters" that heretofore had been the rule, Allen designed what in an irreverent moment he called his "tin desk"; it was to be the first in a long series. Steelcase manufactured a secretarial version of the desk, in steel framed with panels of red, blue, or yellow, that began to appear "by the thousands." The executive desks were designed with ebony matte steel pedestals, polished chrome legs, and solid, butcher-block tops. Cabinets were

ABOVE: On completion, the Inland Steel tower was the first significant new building constructed in Chicago's Loop in more than twenty years.

OPPOSITE TOP: The entry corridor from the elevator lobby to the executive floor. Materials for the furniture and fittings were selected to reflect both the design of the base-building architecture and the steel that was the company's stock-in-trade. Allen's first "tin desk" appeared with pedestals in an ebonized finish.

OPPOSITE BOTTOM: Rough-rolled plate glass partitions framed in stainless steel define the reception area of the executive suite, recalling the detailing of the base building so that "what was true outside became true inside."

ABOVE: Allen's "tin desk," seen in a table version in the chairman's office, was the first modern desk to be manufactured by Steelcase. The clean, crisp effect of teak, glass, and steel in the space expressed the epitome of the 1950's corporate aesthetic.

LEFT: The walnut top of the chairman's table, designed by Allen for the executive dining room, was edged with stainless steel and supported on a four-point base of the same material. Danish chairs completed the ensemble.

RIGHT AND BELOW: Two views of the president's office. The "tin desk" appears in its modified table version with teak butcher-block top and ebonized lacquer pedestals in a frame of polished stainless steel. With the exception of the Danish wood chair, all the furniture was designed by Allen. The traditional shape and shade of the lamp on the seating area's side table indicate that lighting design had not yet caught up with the modern vocabulary of furniture design.

made of teak. From Knoll came Barcelona and early Eero Saarinen chairs; wood side and dining chairs were selected from Georg Jensen's Danish collection.

The interior space was planned with movable partitions for flexible reconfiguration. These partitions and the windows were framed with stainless steel, repeating the exterior material so that "what was true outside became true inside." Remembering his resolution of the Fifth Avenue Manufacturers Hanover executive floor, Allen designed floor-to-ceiling doors with minimal hardware, a process he described as "getting rid of all the trash."

As SOM's first project combining complete interior and furniture design with base building architecture, the Inland Steel headquarters marked a significant milestone in the development of the firm's services. It was no less important for Davis Allen, establishing his place in a team structure that was to become a leading source of corporate design in the years to follow.

ABOVE: The first chair designed by Allen was this executive lounge or side chair constructed with black leather seats encased in an industrial steel mesh frame on slender legs. The chair was used extensively throughout the executive floor at Inland Steel.

OPPOSITE TOP: Allen's surfboard-shaped boardroom table was constructed with a top of laminated solid walnut on double pedestals of polished stainless steel.

OPPOSITE BELOW: The boardroom seating was also designed by Allen. Black leather upholstered chairs were balanced on splayed legs—standard elements in the design vocabulary of the mid-1950s.

CROWN ZELLERBACH,
SAN FRANCISCO, CALIFORNIA, COMPLETED **1959**

PARTNER-IN-CHARGE: JOHN BARNEY RODGERS
DESIGN PARTNER: EDWARD C. BASSETT

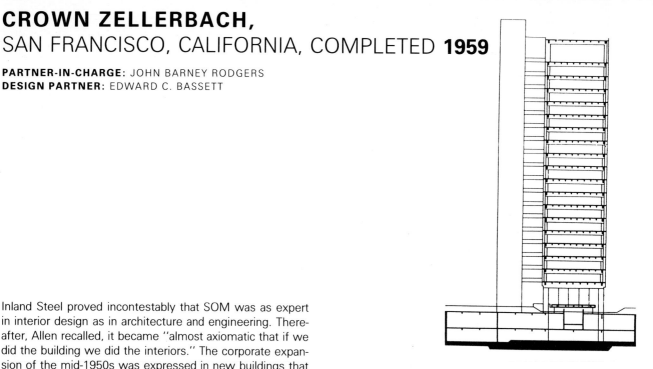

Inland Steel proved incontestably that SOM was as expert in interior design as in architecture and engineering. Thereafter, Allen recalled, it became "almost axiomatic that if we did the building we did the interiors." The corporate expansion of the mid-1950s was expressed in new buildings that bespoke confidence in progress and prosperity. SOM as a foremost exponent of modern design was engaged in a stimulating array of overlapping jobs for corporate clients who wished to project a visible and identifiable image, among them Union Carbide, PepsiCo Inc., and, in what was to be a particularly fruitful association, the Chase Manhattan Bank.

Allen, fresh from his Chicago success, returned to New York to work on the initial stages of the Union Carbide headquarters project (now headquarters of the Manufacturers Hanover Corporation) on Park Avenue, becoming involved in a new branch office for Chase a few blocks farther north as well. At the same time, Nat Owings had secured the commission to design a twenty-story headquarters for the Crown Zellerbach corporation in San Francisco; he requested Allen's services for the interior planning and furniture of the executive floor. Allen was involved primarily as a consultant, working out of New York but making periodic presentations in San Francisco. As he himself noted while reviewing photographs of the project, the resemblance to Inland Steel was more than coincidental, although the secretarial desks bore a strong resemblance to a new piece Allen had designed for Chase. "I was already busy with Chase, and a lot of things seem to have come out of the great stirring of the time," he explained. As Allen's work developed its mature confidence, he explored and expounded on a vocabulary articulating both the firm's and the clients' faith in a refined minimalist aesthetic within an architecturally integrated interior environment. Materials might increase in richness from laminate to marble or from butcher block to rosewood. But the underlying philosophy of sophisticated simplification remained constant: "What was true outside became true inside."

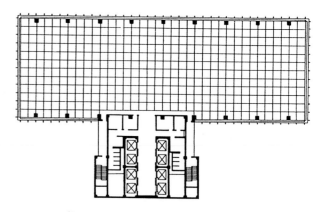

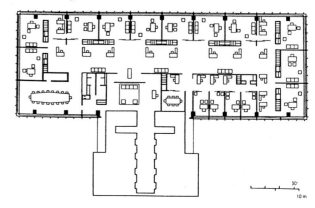

OPPOSITE: The plaza and executive floor in plan, with the tower shown in section.

ABOVE: The twenty-story Crown Zellerbach headquarters in downtown San Francisco.

TOP RIGHT: The cool language of 1950s modernism created an image of confidence and efficiency for corporate America. In "the great stirring of that time," Allen expropriated elements of several projects for the design of the executive floor at Crown Zellerbach. The secretarial desks, for example, were strongly related to the series he was in the process of developing for the Chase Manhattan Bank headquarters, in design at the same time.

CENTER RIGHT: Similarly, the board table and chairs were in the same vocabulary as Allen's recently completed Inland Steel project.

BOTTOM RIGHT: This executive office was in the mainstream of its time, tailored in the SOM interior architecture vernacular which Allen was instrumental in creating.

CHASE MANHATTAN BANK,
410 PARK AVENUE BRANCH,
NEW YORK, NEW YORK, COMPLETED 1959

PARTNER-IN-CHARGE: WALTER SEVERINGHAUS
DESIGN PARTNER: GORDON BUNSHAFT

In concert with the commissioning of the massive sixty-story downtown headquarters for Chase, as much an exercise in city planning as in architecture and engineering, the New York office was engaged to design a smaller, 40,000-square-foot midtown office at 410 Park Avenue. The street and mezzanine floors were to be available to customers for banking transactions, while the fourth floor was reserved for a satellite executive suite.

The timing and size of this job would test SOM's radical proposal that the recently merged Chase National Bank and Bank of Manhattan Company should adopt a contemporary aesthetic as its corporate standard. Gordon Bunshaft took advantage of the occasion to emphasize his belief in art as a decorative element integral to the architectural solution. The architect, together with Museum of Modern Art curator Dorothy Miller, selected twenty pieces by such important contemporary artists as Sam Francis, Charles Burchfield, Jasper Johns, James Brooks, and Alexander Calder. The result was so well received that it became the basis for David Rockefeller's establishment of the bank's corporate art collection, implemented in 1959, which in turn set a precedent for other institutional art programs. *Interiors* magazine called 410 Park Avenue "the epitome of twentieth-century bank design." The art critic Katharine Kuh wrote in *Saturday Review,* "Well chosen, well lighted, these paintings are seen to their best advantage in a setting where color, texture, and space have been intelligently integrated."

Davis Allen, leading the interior design team, recognized that the project represented an unparalleled opportunity and threw himself into it with enthusiasm. It was his first of many collaborations with Gordon Bunshaft in the "intelligent integration" of interior space. The complete range of furniture created for this office was to become the prototype for the furniture in the downtown building. Rich materials were introduced, including marble, rosewood, polished chrome, and silk. A monochromatic palette in the public areas, dominated by a black mobile by Calder, provided a dramatic foil for these materials of contrasting textures. The executive floor was aglow in the warmth of yellow silk walls, tan carpeting, gold curtains, tan leather, and red wool upholstery, a dramatic effect that was heightened by the placement of art at the axes and vistas.

The plan of the executive floor was conceived to provide an informal atmosphere for board meetings, visiting bank officers, and guests. Four private "universal" offices (for use by visitors) lined the entry corridor. Beyond the glass wall at the turn of the corridor was the dining room, and beyond that the boardroom with sofas, club chairs, and glass-topped coffee tables to stress the unconventional air of informality. The floor also included three private dining rooms, a kitchen, and a serving pantry.

Allen's interior planning and furniture design now advanced beyond the ideas formulated for Inland Steel. The desk was refined in order to function more efficiently; there was a greater fluency and finesse in detailing. A splayed chrome table base now supported a rosewood rather than a teak top. The inclusion of works of art in the planning concept fulfilled the vision of total design that Allen had first espoused in Scandinavia, had later noticed in the Cincinnati Terrace Plaza Hotel project as an SOM intern in 1946, and had had the opportunity to implement at Inland Steel. The totality projected confidence in the language of modernism as an appropriate vehicle for defining both the interior and the exterior appearance of buildings. Yet one also served as a foil to the other: while the exterior was sparse, slick, and minimal, the interior was embellished with color, texture, and the splendor of the art of its time.

OPPOSITE: This branch bank and satellite executive office tested the art program and furniture standards established for the new Chase Manhattan Plaza.

RIGHT: The simplicity of the interior design resolution was belied by the richness of its materials, colors, and textures.

BELOW: The fourth floor of 410 Park Avenue was designed for the use of senior officers visiting from the downtown headquarters, and contained office/meeting rooms, an informal lounge boardroom, and dining facilities. The marble and rosewood reception desk clearly shows that, with the advent of the decade of the 1960s, a more sophisticated language was evolving from 1950s modernism.

35

LEFT: The platform area on the ground floor was separated from the public space by an elongated file bank topped with marble.

BELOW: A dramatic mural by Sam Francis dominated the lounge area on the fourth floor, where the board held meetings in informal surroundings.

ABOVE: The scale of the mezzanine banking hall is indicated by the twenty-foot span of Alexander Calder's black mobile. Teller counters on two sides of the space were detailed to complement the elegance of the freestanding check-writing console. The marble-faced paneling ran the entire height of both ground and mezzanine floors.

RIGHT: Yellow silk wallcovering and full-length curtains created a warm environment in the fourth-floor dining room, where cantilevered credenzas supported sculpture selected from the recently established Chase Fine Arts Program.

LEFT: The informality of the boardroom lounge was continued in the executive dining room.

BELOW: Mies van der Rohe Barcelona chairs, upholstered in tan leather, were introduced to the ground floor platform area, supplementing rows of Allen desks in teak and stainless steel, with black upholstered pull-up chairs.

BELOW: Four private rooms were
provided on the fourth floor off the
reception area for use as "off-site" offices
or meeting rooms by visiting bank
officers. The rooms were separated from
the circulation corridor by sliding door
partitions of sandblasted glass.

CHASE MANHATTAN PLAZA,
NEW YORK, NEW YORK, COMPLETED **1961**

PARTNER-IN-CHARGE: WALTER SEVERINGHAUS
DESIGN PARTNER: GORDON BUNSHAFT

By the mid-1950s, Park Avenue was luring the captains of industry to the glamour and convenience of a midtown address. The Chase Manhattan Bank's commitment to construct its new headquarters in the Wall Street area thus signaled a revival of faith in the downtown financial district. The indefatigable Nat Owings proposed that Chase's building become the cornerstone of a reconstruction program that would revitalize a moribund area of buildings verging on obsolesence.

The solution that SOM offered included the creation of a 2.5-acre site by closing a city street and thereby joining two blocks. The tower would be set back on a plaza, bringing a welcome modicum of open space to the tightly knit pattern of narrow streets. The entire space would encompass more than 2 million square feet: 1.8 million square feet in the tower and the remainder below plaza grade. Chase initially was to occupy thirty-seven of the sixty floors. The plan provided for a banking hall, staff cafeteria, general floors divided among clerical areas, facilities for private banking, and offices for 137 vice presidents. Amenities of the executive suites on the seventeenth floor included a barber shop and an express elevator to the sixtieth-floor dining room.

The project began in 1955 and continued for six years. The talent and energy of Davis Allen swung into high gear as the teams of architects, engineers, and interior designers were orchestrated under the overall direction of Gordon Bunshaft. The exercises in furniture design for 410 Park Avenue were now standardized for larger-scale production. Such was the scope of the project that the interiors team designed a vast multiplicity of accessories, including bathroom taps and fittings that the manufacturer, American Standard, adopted for its line.

The accolades for the art at the Park Avenue branch led to the establishment of a full-scale Fine Arts Program for the collection of original works of painting and sculpture focused on, but not limited to, the twentieth century. A committee of experts was formed to vote on possible acquisitions. Davis Allen attended these meetings as assistant to Bun-

shaft, who was a voting member of the committee. The welcome result, Allen recalled, was that "I got to go out shopping a lot!"

But shopping was a minor distraction from the concentration of effort required in order to plan, furnish, and integrate art into thirty-seven floors of what Christopher Woodward in a 1970 book on SOM called "the apotheosis of SOM design." The executive floor and the dining rooms atop the sixtieth floor received the particular benefit of Allen's expertise in spatial and decorative artistry. *Architectural Forum* remarked on "the board room with sixty chairs, a single vast table, and one Soulages painting almost 5 feet square on the end wall."

OPPOSITE: The sixty-story Chase Manhattan Plaza represented a major turning point in the development of New York's downtown financial district.

TOP RIGHT: On the mezzanine banking platform, rows of teak and stainless steel desks, first seen in the 410 Park Avenue branch, were joined by a new version of Allen's marble and black lacquer reception desk with panels running to the floor.

CENTER RIGHT: Tufted leather sofas and lounge chairs, designed by Allen, furnished the seventeenth-floor executive lounge. The painting is by Jose Guerrero.

BOTTOM RIGHT: Private customer areas were denoted by carpeted floors. The standard Allen-designed desks were detailed with black lacquer front and side panels for a slightly more elaborate and elegant flourish.

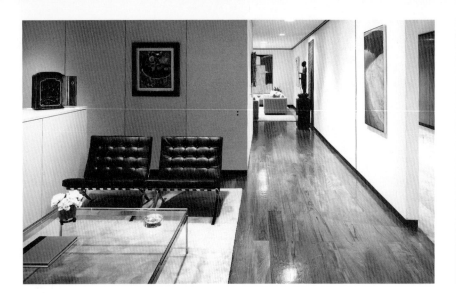

The chairman's office was an immense thirty-by-thirty-foot expanse of white walls and teak flooring, with furniture arranged in three configurations: a desk, informal seating, and an area for conferences. The art for the suite included a highly eclectic assortment of pieces by Kenzo Okada, Adolph Gottlieb, Milton Avery, Charles Burchfield, Jose Guerrero, Josef Albers, and Jean Dubuffet, while the chairman's anteroom was dominated by a superb painting by Mark Rothko. A corner étagère contained a selection of books, small carvings, sculpture, and artifacts.

Some years later, Charles Pfister, at the time a brilliant young interior designer at SOM San Francisco and today president of The Pfister Partnership, an *Interiors* magazine Designer of the Year, and a member of the *Interior Design* magazine Hall of Fame, visited David Rockefeller's office in the company of Davis Allen. The office had been repainted and the chairman had requested Allen to come and replace the objects in their original position on the étagère, as no one else could remember exactly how they had been arranged. Pfister said, "Dave quickly put everything in order, stepped back, and with a conspiratorial smile said, 'Now will somebody be so kind as to take a picture so you don't have to get me down here every time you repaint.'" As they left, Allen remarked to Pfister, "Well, I guess you can't be a nanny to a building forever."

Raul de Armas, who joined SOM in 1967, is an *Interiors* magazine Designer of the Year and now the partner in the New York office most involved with interior design. He refers to the Chase chairman's office as "the high point of the modern vocabulary at SOM. If you move the furniture three inches the space doesn't work. Without the art, the space doesn't function. What Dave Allen created was not just a room with furniture, but a cool and extremely architectural melange of three rooms in one."

Never again would SOM with such insouciance give form to the Miesian philosophy of the minimalist envelope perfectly offset by textured materials, furniture placed in rigorously controlled formation, and art objects chosen and presented with impeccable taste. The opening of the 1960s produced a sense that strict Bauhausian discipline had run its course and would require refocusing if the style was not to become a mindless cliché. Rather than rejecting or negating the accomplishments of the past, SOM preferred to layer and expand upon its heritage. The Chase headquarters, far from marking the end of an era, thus represented a point of departure, leading to further evolution of the SOM interior vocabulary. It was the mold from which the aesthetic expressed in the work of Davis Allen was shaped and a source from which the firm continues to draw inspiration and enlightenment.

ABOVE AND OPPOSITE: The design of the chairman's office demonstrates Allen's masterful integration of furniture, works of art, and decorative objects within an envelope of white walls and teak floors. ABOVE LEFT: The reception anteroom. ABOVE RIGHT: Looking back from the office interior to the anteroom. OPPOSITE TOP: A private conference area was part of the chairman's suite. OPPOSITE: The seating area at the entry to the thirty-by-thirty-foot space, in which a Japanese wood-carved figure is on display.

LEFT: Executive officers were allowed to select furniture and artwork from the corporate standards program to furnish their own offices. The result was a controlled variety of individual tastes and preferences on the seventeenth floor of the building. TOP: The office of this executive revealed a penchant for wood. A marble-topped conference table on a polished stainless steel base and a centered Davis Allen desk were selected. CENTER: A circular marble-topped table on a stainless steel base became this officer's desk, with sled-base Brno pull-up chairs and a glass-topped, stainless steel coffee table in the seating area. BOTTOM: Wood and marble were also selected by this executive officer, who placed his Allen desk close to the window view.

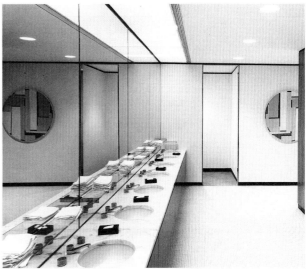

TOP LEFT: An example of Allen's ability to maintain continuity within the framework of the SOM vocabulary is the table he designed for the executive conference room on the seventeenth floor. By specifying marble in place of the laminated walnut top of the original, he gave new life to an enduring concept.

TOP RIGHT: Works of art and teak paneling were not precluded from the executive bathroom on the sixtieth floor. Sink fittings were designed by the SOM interiors team.

ABOVE: An elegant antique hunt table-desk and chairs contrasted with a modern sofa and lounge chairs in this Chase executive's office.

BUSINESSMEN'S ASSURANCE COMPANY OF AMERICA,
KANSAS CITY, MISSOURI, COMPLETED **1963**

DESIGN PARTNER: BRUCE J. GRAHAM

BELOW: Situated at the head of the Santa Fe Trail, the project was embellished with Native American artifacts and, in a private executive office, a bovine weather vane saluting a prime product of the Midwest.

As the Chase project wound down, the Chicago office requested that Davis Allen assist in the interior design of a nineteen-story tower set on a hill overlooking Kansas City. The location, at the head of the Santa Fe Trail, suggested a Native American motif to the Midwestern Allen, who was thus inspired to travel west in order to find "Indian things" to complete the interior scheme. In contrast to the high sophistication of the art selected for Inland Steel and Chase, the Businessmen's Assurance Company collection demonstrated Allen's appreciation of the folkloric and primitive. He assembled a collection from sources as diverse as the Santa Fe Museum and small shops: arrowheads mounted in a decorative pattern and framed, Navaho jewelry displayed in a vitrine coffee table, and Apache baskets and blankets hung with the reverence generally accorded antique tapestries.

Although the furniture was largely in the Chase vernacular, a natural choice given the timing of the project, these interiors could be distinguished by Allen's evolving ability to meld objects of contrasting periods and values in eclectic and successful combination.

Davis Allen has the rare ability to recognize intrinsic worth: a trinket found in a hotel gift shop or a shell or stone picked up on a beach can be positioned comfortably alongside a priceless antique. "I never placed a money value on things. I was more interested in their visual value. I might have known that it cost a great deal, but if it cost twenty-five cents or if I picked it up off the ground it didn't make any difference." Allen's next project, the complete interior design of the Mauna Kea Beach Hotel in Hawaii, would demonstrate the remarkable intensity of this commitment to the integrity of intrinsic beauty.

RIGHT: Kachina dolls from New Mexico created a playful atmosphere in the executive dining room. The Navaho blanket on display was borrowed from a Santa Fe museum.

BELOW: Native American figurines stood on leather file boxes designed by Allen for the chairman's office.

TOP: Indian baskets were hung on the wall of the executive floor reception area above a Western Pioneer box recalling the adventuresome days of the trek into the Great Plains and beyond.

ABOVE: The executive desk was developed from the reception desk designed for the Chase Manhattan Bank project. Allen mounted and framed a collection of Indian arrowheads to decorate the wall.

TOP LEFT: Allen ingeniously suggested a stone cart wheel as a sculptural element placed against a red Southwestern blanket at the entry to the executive floor reception area.

TOP RIGHT: In the boardroom, the folkloric simplicity of an overscaled Apache basket was contrasted with the sophistication of the marble and polished stainless steel of the Allen table and red upholstered chairs.

ABOVE: The Chase influence was continued here in the chairman's antique hunt table-desk and Danish chairs. A collection of Navaho jewelry was displayed in the vitrine table.

MAUNA KEA BEACH HOTEL,
KAMUELA, HAWAII, COMPLETED **1965**

PARTNER-IN-CHARGE: NATHANIEL OWINGS
DESIGN PARTNER: EDWARD C. BASSETT

To their credit, SOM partners recognized that Davis Allen's genius, and indeed his genial personality, could best be employed as a firmwide resource rather than as a fixed entity confined to a particular office or circumscribed management duties. He was perceived and appreciated as the ultimate interior designer. The Chase project instilled confidence among the partners that Allen would continue to respect the founding principles of the "Gothic Builders Guild"; thereafter he was freed to create the environments that came to establish the firm's interior design methodology.

In 1963 Allen was brought onto the team that Nat Owings and Edward C. Bassett were assembling in San Francisco to complete the design for a 150-room resort hotel on the Kona Coast of the island of Hawaii. Allen was entrusted with total responsibility for the interior furnishings and design of the building. Allen regards this project, under the aegis of Laurance Rockefeller, as the most significant and personally satisfying of his career, "A unique, exciting chance in that it was nothing like what I had been doing up to then in steel and glass buildings." Allen now drew upon his encyclopedic memory to recall those elegant spaces and decorative embellishments, fashioned over centuries, with which he had become acquainted during his extensive travels in Mediterranean countries and Europe. His concept for Mauna Kea was based on the informality and ease of a large country house, combined with the refined atmosphere of a European grand hotel. It would reflect the traditions and arts not just of Hawaii but of the entire Pacific Basin, from Japan, India, and Southeast Asia to Samoa, Tonga, New Zealand, and New Guinea.

Such a universal concept was a revelation to the young designer assigned to work with Allen. Margo Grant, now a member of the *Interior Design* magazine Hall of Fame, Vice President of the prestigious Gensler and Associates and Managing Principal of its New York and London offices, had joined SOM San Francisco in 1960, fresh from the University of Oregon. Three years later, upon finally meeting this man who was spoken of with such enormous respect, she was astonished to be told that she was to be his lieutenant for the project and was to accompany him on a tour of existing hotels in the Hawaiian Islands. Allen had laid down this stipulation before starting work on the project, so that a frame of reference could be established. Hawaii was thought of in terms of muumuus, leis, and garish shirts, and "Dave believed that there must be something else there. I was stunned," Grant recalled,

> because I wasn't used to anyone thinking that big. He was thinking of the overall concept, but he was also thinking of the details. I'd never known, in school or in my work experience, anyone who approached design the way Dave did. When I first met him, he was already considered the dean of the designers in the firm. I held him in great awe in the beginning, but as we got acquainted on the trip I found him to be such a warm and straightforward no-pretense person, and we formed a friendship."

Allen's approach was based partly on intuition, partly on his habit of observation, and partly on his innate Midwestern common sense. "I had friends from Yale whose ancestors had been missionaries in Hawaii, so I had some contacts there." he recalled.

OPPOSITE TOP: The Mauna Kea Beach Hotel, sited on almost 500 acres on Hawaii's Big Island, has been acclaimed as one of the world's finest resorts.

OPPOSITE BOTTOM: Allen resourcefully created "art" from shells collected on the Mauna Kea beaches, mounting them on red and yellow backgrounds framed in white wood for each of the 150 guest rooms. Allen also designed the willow furniture which he had manufactured in Italy.

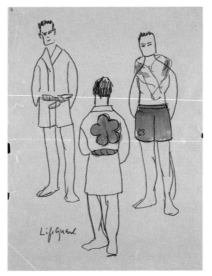

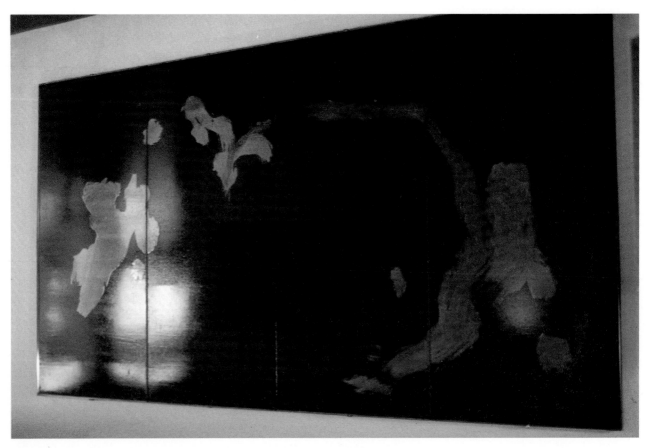

TOP: Although never executed, Allen's sketches for the design of captain, lifeguard, and maid uniforms indicate his thorough approach at Mauna Kea, his most significant and satisfying project.

ABOVE: A four-panel, lacquered screen by the Japanese calligrapher and artist Morita Shiyu was hung on the wall of the main elevator lobby. The legend reads: "A Dragon Knows Dragon."

TOP LEFT: The plumeria is one of Hawaii's most abundant blossoms. Allen suggested a stylized version of the flower, in reddish orange, as the hotel's logo, used on all graphic materials.

TOP RIGHT: A large gilt fish from Thailand overlooks the inner court of the building.

ABOVE: The Garuda, an eighteenth-century Ayudhya figure reputedly blessed with superhuman qualities, sits majestically in the main lobby. The figure is carved and decorated with polychrome mirror mosaic.

When I went there with Margo, I wanted to get a feeling for the whole place, so I asked them to show us the most beautiful houses, gardens, the nicest hotels and restaurants, clubs, museums, and even hospitals to see what the expectations were. I used this same approach later on other projects.

From my point of view, none of the hotels had the feeling that one should have in Mauna Kea, and I wanted to change that. I wanted this thing to look like a house, and to make it casual and unpretentious. I made a proposal to Laurance Rockefeller and gave him an idea of how much money we would need; it was less than one hundred thousand dollars. He okayed it, and said that I could spend even more if I needed to. I went off on a seven-week shopping trip to Hong Kong, Thailand, India, and Japan.

Allen shopped in museums, street markets, department stores, hotel gift shops, arts-and-crafts studios, and workshops. In Kyoto, he ran into John McGuire, head of a San Francisco furniture company, who introduced him to a Japanese friend who agreed to guide Allen to antique and lacquer shops. In Bangkok, Allen met the legendary adventurer and textile entrepreneur Jim Thompson, who led him to a source of Thai antiques and to a Shan princess on the Burmese-Chinese border who wove the bedspreads for all 150 rooms. Upholstery for the willow furniture that McGuire made to Allen's specifications was specially woven in Thailand. Other objects were ordered by correspondence from Allen's global network of friends and contacts as far afield as Zanzibar and Tunisia, while bar chairs by Vico Magistretti were obtained through Terence Conran's Habitat furnishing shop in London.

Allen came back with more than a thousand "charming, mysterious, glamorous things," wrote Nat Owings, turning Mauna Kea "into a luxury palace." The designer's intention was to form a collection "of decorative objects—things we like that are interesting, some of museum quality." In spite of this modest disclaimer, after more than twenty-five years the Mauna Kea collection has come to be recognized as one of the most important contributions ever made to the understanding and appreciation of the complexity and range of Pacific Basin cultures.

The serendipity continued in Hawaii itself, where Allen and Grant came upon the quilt makers of the Kawaihoa Mission Church. In Grant's recollection, "These women were making quilts in wonderful sorts of Easter egg colors; Dave immediately recognized their marvelous design of beautiful patterns and vivid colors." Laurance Rockefeller, who at Allen's suggestion commissioned thirty quilts to be hung as tapestries throughout the hotel corridors, is thereby credited with reviving an art that was on the verge of extinction. Allen collected seashells from Pacific beaches; mounted and framed, they became guest-room "pictures." A local artist was commissioned to execute a Flowers of Hawaii series. Allen took the originals to Mourlot, a Parisian lithographer who had worked with Picasso; a set of lithographs was made and framed. "Only Dave Allen would have thought of this," Grant said: "To see flowers in Hawaii, commission watercolors of them, and have them made as prints halfway around the world in Paris. But one of Dave's secrets is his ability to see things that other people don't."

In the Mauna Kea project, Grant said, "All of Dave's talents were used as they probably haven't been used again. He was able to take that attention to detail and weave all those eclectic objects into one design. He had no preconceived ideas but brought all the fine and interesting things he'd seen in so many places into one place. He is such an observer and his taste is so exquisite. No one else could have done it."

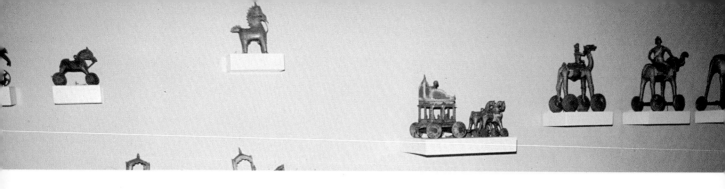

ABOVE, BELOW, AND OPPOSITE: Davis Allen's global search for decorative objects he considered "interesting" resulted in a collection that reflected the cultural heritage of the entire Pacific region. Among them: (clockwise from bottom left): A brass parrot cage found in Hong Kong; Head masks from New Guinea, worn for the yam ceremony ritual, mounted on tree fern trunks in the promenade elevator lobby; A tiered brass Indian candelabra, formerly used in a Hindu temple, in the dining pavilion; An eighteenth-century Japanese wooden horse, traditionally ridden by children during festivals; A collection of temple toys from India, mounted on shelves at various levels of the fifth-floor guest room elevator lobby.

RIGHT: Upholstery fabric for the lobby settees designed by Allen was woven in Thailand, while the furniture was manufactured in Italy.

BELOW: One of the collection of thirty hand-stitched kapas made by the quiltmakers of Honolulu's Kawaiahao Mission Church. The commission by Laurance Rockefeller was credited with reviving a languishing folk art of the Hawaiian Islands.

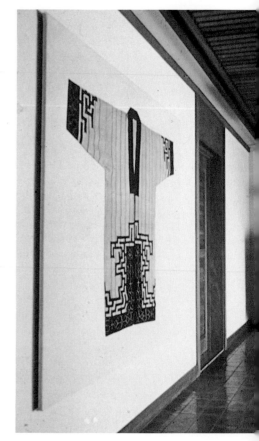

RIGHT: The elaborate willow settee in the elevator lobby on the fifth floor was designed by Davis Allen and made in Hong Kong.

BELOW: A rare Ainu kimono, one of four collected by Allen for Mauna Kea, was used as a wall hanging. Research suggests that the Ainu tribe of the Japanese island Hokkaido may have migrated from Polynesia to Japan centuries ago.

BELOW RIGHT: In the main elevator lobby, a Japanese barn hook (jizai) was mounted as a piece of sculpture and displayed on a tansu table also from Japan.

MARINE MIDLAND BANK,
NEW YORK, NEW YORK, COMPLETED **1967**

PARTNER-IN-CHARGE: EDWARD J. MATTHEWS
DESIGN PARTNER: GORDON BUNSHAFT

ABOVE: The scale of the furniture
designed for the banking hall respects the
lofty proportions of the space. The leather
sofa and lounge chairs were placed on a
carpet of brilliant red, perhaps referring to
the color of the Noguchi cube on the
plaza outside.

TOP: Davis Allen continued to expound upon his "tin desk" theme as seen in a large-scale version for the officers' platforms.

ABOVE: Compared with his earlier projects, Allen began to introduce a more traditional and "clubby" feeling to the executive office. This trend would continue to evolve as the decade of the 1970s approached.

The Marine Midland Bank was the anchor tenant of this fifty-story speculative building at 140 Broadway, New York City, occupying ten floors above and two floors below a plaza upon which stands a twenty-eight-foot-tall red Noguchi cube balanced on the point of a single corner. Bunshaft's biographer, Carol Herselle Krinsky, notes that Davis Allen's interior concept not only "matched the scale of the spaces, from the eighteen-foot-high banking hall to the lower and smaller spaces in the upper stories" but also "relieved the neutral tones of the walls and floors with luxurious materials and textures and bright colors."

Perhaps emboldened by the bravura of Mauna Kea, Allen here moved away from the intentionally reserved palette of his earlier work to a more exuberant interior vocabulary. He also began to introduce a traditional residential ambience to the corporate environment, emphasized in the leather Chesterfield sofa and matching armchairs designed for the banking hall and the president's office. The space of that office was defined into specific areas by freestanding storage elements, breaking with the open plan used in the chairman's office at Chase. The introduction of clear green and red carpeting was another indication that the winds of change were blowing in with the turbulent mid-1960s. In the context of Davis Allen's career, this transitional project is therefore of particular interest.

NATIONAL LIFE AND ACCIDENT COMPANY,
NASHVILLE, TENNESSEE, COMPLETED **1970**

PARTNER-IN-CHARGE: WILLIAM HARTMANN
DESIGN PARTNER: BRUCE J. GRAHAM

Consulting with SOM Chicago, Davis Allen was drafted once again to soften an executive environment, this time in the twenty-eight-story National Life and Accident Company building in Nashville, Tennessee. Working with Allen on the project was Margaret McCurry, who would later become the partner and wife of architect Stanley Tigerman.

The company's executives had acknowledged some trepidation at the prospect of moving from their traditional southern-style building across the street. The light touch of Davis Allen was therefore indispensable to their happy transition from a familiar environment into a contemporary tower. He cushioned the shock of the new by including several pieces of antique furniture from the former address, as well as bringing over the company's carved American eagle to preside over the boardroom. Along the travertine-floored corridor to the executive suite, Allen placed Moroccan rugs purchased on a trip to Rabat, even matching them with one bought at Bloomingdale's in New York! The residential ambience of the executive spaces was orchestrated without compromising the modern spirit of the architecture expressed in the travertine walls and interior steelmullion detailing as well as in the scale of the furniture.

Two elements of the project were to have a lasting effect on the Skidmore vocabulary. The first was the folding gridded sunscreen designed to shade the boardroom from the hot southern sun without closing off the view of the Tennessee hills from its floor-to-ceiling windows. "It didn't matter if you were sitting at the table or standing up; you could still see the outside without the sun in your eyes," Allen said. The second was the appearance of Allen's first spindle chair, which he had designed the year before for the Texas Bank and Trust Company, Dallas. Allen's preoccupation with the grace, proportions, and material of the Windsor chair would be further developed in the furniture he designed in the 1980s, most notably his Andover and Bridgehampton chairs, which became instant classics and have been used extensively in SOM projects in the postmodern genre.

OPPOSITE: In a design solution that can truly be called "transitional," Allen began to soften the angles and minimalism of strict Miesian modernism without compromising the building's integral architectural elements.

TOP RIGHT: The curved lines of plush upholstered guest seating in the executive anteroom conveyed an aura of warm Southern hospitality in the context of contemporary architecture.

CENTER RIGHT: Travertine walls and floors in the executive reception area maintained the integrity of the building's architecture.

BOTTOM RIGHT: The restraint of a muted palette brought distinction to the executive dining room on the penthouse floor of the National Life project.

LEFT: A storage cube/occasional table was designed for executive use by Allen in rich leather with brass trim.

BELOW: Rugs purchased by Allen in Morocco were used extensively in the space. The rug in this corridor, however, was one bought at Bloomingdale's!

OPPOSITE TOP: Allen's first spindle chair appeared in the National Life project. His interest in the American tradition of wood was to continue into the 1990s.

OPPOSITE BOTTOM: Allen designed this folding honeycomb-gridded screen for the boardroom. It was to become a signature element of the SOM interior vernacular.

AMERICAN CAN COMPANY,
GREENWICH, CONNECTICUT, COMPLETED **1970**

DESIGN PARTNER: GORDON BUNSHAFT
PROJECT MANAGER: FREDERICK C. GANS, ASSOCIATE PARTNER

GENERAL ELECTRIC COMPANY,
FAIRFIELD, CONNECTICUT, COMPLETED **1975**

DESIGN PARTNER: ROY ALLEN
PROJECT MANAGER: FREDERICK C. GANS, ASSOCIATE PARTNER

ABOVE: The executive suites of the American Can Company were housed in a separate single-story structure with a central courtyard adjacent to the main block of general offices.

LEFT: The visitor seating area in the American Can executive building enjoyed the benefit of views to the interior courtyard.

These two projects, completed within a period of five years, were designed on suburban sites in residential neighborhoods and therefore required extreme sensitivity to the surrounding landscape and community sensibilities.

The architectural plans are similar: a three-story main office structure with an adjoining but detached single-story structure accommodating executive areas designed around an interior court. There is an assured, country-club feel to the furnishing of both interiors; Allen adopted a residential vocabulary in order to convey a sense of ease and business as usual.

ABOVE: The General Electric Company headquarters followed the siting concept that had worked successfully for American Can. The quality of the interior plan was considerably enhanced by the ability to "borrow" natural light from two sources: the courtyard and the building perimeter.

LEFT: Seating in the main reception area of the General Electric headquarters was upholstered in red and placed in a "conversation pit" arrangement around a generously scaled reception desk.

LEFT: American Can staff cafeteria amenities included a tree-surrounded lakeside view, and a promenade deck for seasonal alfresco dining and strolling.

BELOW: The chairman's office was elegantly appointed in an eclectic mix of the traditional and transitional, with a Japanese screen as the focal point.

RIGHT: Executive offices were placed around the perimeter of the General Electric headquarters. Interior offices were arranged within low partitions so that "borrowed light" from the exterior could be drawn inward.

BELOW: To facilitate the circulation of light, glass partitions enclosed the perimeter private offices, including the chairman's office shown here.

LYNDON BAINES JOHNSON LIBRARY,
AUSTIN, TEXAS, COMPLETED 1971

DESIGN PARTNER: GORDON BUNSHAFT
PROJECT MANAGER: FREDERICK C. GANS, ASSOCIATE PARTNER

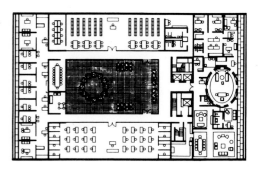

SOM's New York office was called upon to design the monumental, eight-story Lyndon Baines Johnson Library on the University of Texas campus at Austin. Davis Allen was put in charge of creating private quarters and offices on the top floor for the personal use of the retired President and Mrs. Johnson, including a seven-eighths scale replica of the White House Oval Office. In meetings in New York and at the Johnson ranch, Allen got to know the clients' tastes and expectations, which he would later translate into a design solution appropriate to the status of a former President and at the same time reflective of the larger-than-life yet down-home Texan personality of the man himself. The warmth and graciousness of Mrs. Johnson were also taken into account, since she obviously was to share the space, would serve as hostess at social events in the living and dining rooms, and would have her own office.

Allen was accompanied on weekend excursions to the ranch by Carol Groh, who was assigned to the project as his assistant. Groh, today the founding principal of Carol Groh & Associates and an *Interiors* magazine Designer of the Year, was, like Margo Grant before her, still in her twenties and equally intimidated by Allen's "guru" reputation. But she soon found that Allen "was the most gentle person to work with, so good about other people's feelings and never coming on strong. The thing that impressed me most was that from the first meeting with the Johnsons in New York he included me in everything as a peer. That was unheard of in my experience up to then."

Hair-raising high-speed drives around the ranch with Mr. Johnson at the wheel of his Lincoln Continental convertible with the Secret Service in hot pursuit were interspersed with quiet discussions with Mrs. Johnson about her husband and their lives together. Allen took it all in, and in Groh's opinion "designed a lasting, classic environment" that was both presidential and extremely personal. The color palette resonated with the radiance of the flowers that Mrs. Johnson loved, from the "punch of orange red" in her Davis Allen GF desk, to the yellow upholstered Brno chairs in the dining

room, to the Chinese red lacquer-walled anteroom hung with silver-framed photographs of heads of state. Gifts the Johnsons received during his presidency were displayed throughout the suite, some in specially designed étagères. The pens with which the former President had signed landmark bills were laid on red velvet beneath the glass top of the coffee table. Looking back, Groh said she believes that the entire project underscored "Dave's mastery with objects and his ability to bring so many different things together into a marvelously integrated design."

ABOVE: The top floor in plan, with the presidential suite (including a scale replica of the Oval Office), staff offices, and lounges.

OPPOSITE TOP: The sitting room in the presidential suite. A selection of gifts received by the President and his wife were displayed in specially designed étagères.

OPPOSITE BOTTOM: President and Mrs. Johnson's private quarters were situated atop the monolithic library structure.

LEFT: The dining alcove opened off the sitting room. Brno chairs covered in a clear yellow fabric brought a snap of warm color to the space. Many of the colors chosen for the private quarters reflected Mrs. Johnson's well-known love of flowers.

BELOW: Accents of red added zest to the dignity of the Presidential library. Mrs. Johnson's writing desk in red lacquer and bronze was adapted from Allen's existing GF Series.

MARINE MIDLAND CENTER,
BUFFALO, NEW YORK, COMPLETED **1974**

PARTNER-IN-CHARGE: JOHN MERRILL
DESIGN PARTNER: MARC GOLDSTEIN

Called as a consultant to the San Francisco office for the forty-story Marine Midland Center in Buffalo, Davis Allen worked once again with Margo Grant, who by now had gained recognition among the increasingly large and talented group of interior designers at the firm. Allen's ongoing interest in furniture design had led him to refine the concepts that began with the "tin desk" at Inland Steel as further developed for Chase. This thinking brought about a new line of desks and storage cubes in steel and wood that became the Davis Allen GF Collection and Cube Component Series.

The front panels of the earlier desks had stopped above the floor, revealing the occupant's feet, wastebasket, and the telephone and other wires indispensable in the emerging electronic work environment. The logical conclusion, begun in the Chase desks, was to extend the front panel to the floor while concealing support wiring within raceways engineered into the frame, thus contributing to a tidier office landscape. With the GF series, a further step forward was the use of bright, primary-colored steel panels in single- and double-pedestal desks, tables, and credenzas adaptable for executive or secretarial tasks. In the executive version, the steel frame was overlaid with burl oak for a more formal presentation. With its intense colors, the new desk became an important graphic element in Allen's overall design resolution on the general office floors. In the Marine Midland Center, Grant noted, the desk was "the cornerstone of the project; we used it throughout."

The Marine Midland project reflected the prevailing interest in Pop and Op art; Allen encouraged Jim Hill, the San Francisco office's graphic designer, to create supergraphic signage for the elevator lobbies and a large-scale Op pattern for the fiberglass proscenium curtain in the auditorium. The cooperation of the art patron Seymour Knox, a member of the Marine Midland board who had commissioned SOM New York to design the nearby Albright-Knox Art Gallery addition in 1962, resulted in the assemblage of a noteworthy art collection. Allen recalls "a very receptive client. We even designed the chinaware for the executive dining rooms."

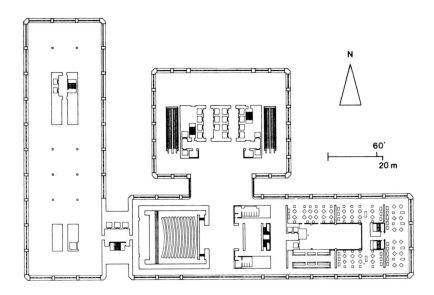

OPPOSITE TOP: Allen's furniture was used "from top to bottom" of the Marine Midland Bank's forty-story headquarters.

OPPOSITE BOTTOM: The executive version of Davis Allen's GF desk was finished in English burl oak for a more formal presentation.

ABOVE: An L-shaped ancilliary building flanks the forty-story tower set upon a plaza site. The second floor, shown in plan, contains the auditorium, cafeteria, and office space.

RIGHT: The GF series of office furniture was designed to cover a variety of end uses. Here the table-desk expresses executive status.

BELOW: An example of a scale model prepared for client presentations and study by the SOM teams. The models typically show spatial and furniture configuration in addition to color and material swatches.

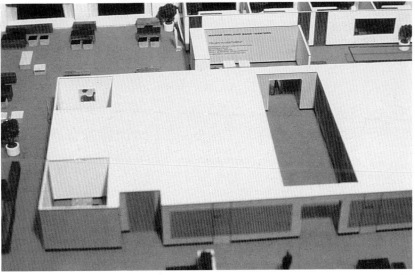

As studies later in the decade would show, enhancement of employee satisfaction in the workplace increases productivity. By turning away from grays and dark woods toward colors and materials suggesting a lighter, more upscale mood, this project was influential in stimulating the introduction of bright colors into the office landscape.

OVERLEAF LEFT: Executive dining rooms on the top floor of the tower afforded vistas of the city below. Chinaware was specifically designed for the project by the SOM team.

OVERLEAF RIGHT, TOP: The adjoining executive lounge was arranged with clubby comfort and designed for informal discussion or serious business.

OVERLEAF RIGHT, BOTTOM: The Fiberglas proscenium curtain for the auditorium was designed in a supergraphic Op art style. Allen's grid-patterned window screens were adapted as a wall treatment, controlling rear-projected ambient lighting.

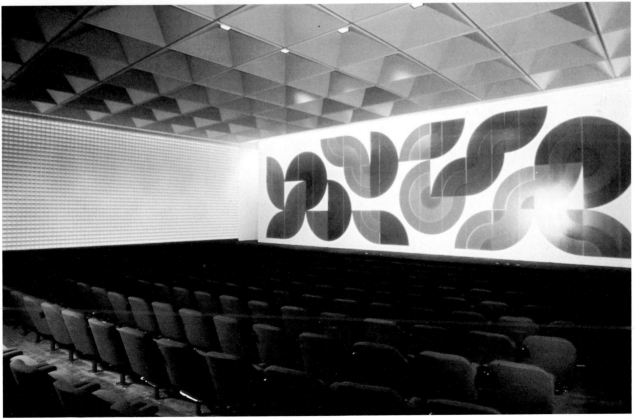

AGNELLI SUITE, TOUR FIAT,
LA DEFENSE, PARIS, COMPLETED **1975**

PARTNER-IN CHARGE: DAVID HUGHES
DESIGN PARTNER: WHITSON OVERCASH

The Agnelli suite atop the forty-four-story Tour Fiat at La De-fense in Paris distilled the essence of elegance into ultra-simplicity. Designed for the personal use of the brothers Gi-anni and Umberto Agnelli on their visits to Paris, it functioned as a pied-à-terre with bedroom, bathroom, and sauna; execu-tive offices and boardroom; and rooms for entertaining both small and large groups. Materials and colors were selected to complement an existing art collection. Although the space was less than 10,000 square feet, the plan conveyed a sense of palatial proportions.

Reached by a spherical private elevator whose walls were faced with red velvet, a regal entry gallery of polished traver-tine ran the entire length of the main axis. This vista was punctuated with a row of columns and doors covered with polished stainless steel. The floor-to-ceiling doors were a majestic five feet wide, opening from the gallery to two pri-vate offices, the boardroom, and conference and dining rooms. These rooms, divided by travertine panels, were set back from the building's perimeter, creating an internal "pal-ace corridor" for private access and communication. Folding sunscreens of white lacquered wood, first used in the Nash-ville project five years earlier, lined the window walls, while pale wool carpeting was laid on the teak floors.

Carol Groh, who worked with Allen on the project, consid-ers it "absolutely cutting edge for its time. It was slick but not slick. It was a jewel." In the lexicon of seminal SOM interiors projects, the Tour Fiat is viewed by many in the firm as a milestone in the measured recessional from high mod-ernism toward a more traditional vernacular. Unfortunately, this lovely space now exists only in photographs. SOM did create a similar example of distilled minimalism in travertine and polished stainless steel almost ten years later in Raul de Armas' design for the reception area of the firm's New York office, thus perpetuating Davis Allen's original contribution.

ABOVE: Incomparable views of Paris were seen from the Agnelli Suite, with Allen's folding sunscreen, designed for the National Life project in Nashville, making its European debut.

TOP LEFT: A private elevator, lined with red velvet walls, transported passengers from the floor below to the spectacular gallery of the suite.

TOP RIGHT: The scale of the gallery was matched perfectly to the magnificent Henry Moore sculpture on the long axis.

ABOVE: Cylindrical columns sheathed in polished stainless steel punctuate the processional space, faced by floor-to-ceiling stainless steel doors set flush against travertine walls.

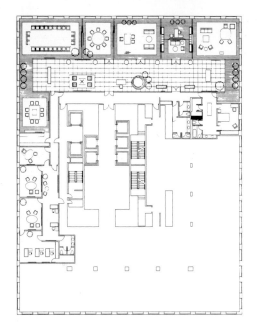

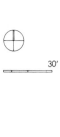

30'

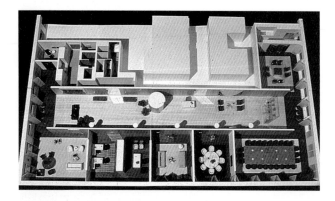

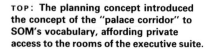

TOP: The planning concept introduced the concept of the "palace corridor" to SOM's vocabulary, affording private access to the rooms of the executive suite.

ABOVE: Scale model of the Agnelli Suite indicates the furniture plan and materials.

ABOVE: Modern Paris in the 1970s was confined to a controversial new high-rise development called La Defense. The forty-four-story Tour Fiat was just one of several new structures built on the western edge of the city in that period.

OPPOSITE TOP: The walls and floor of the suite's private bathroom, which contained a sauna in addition to the more expected amenities, were sheathed in travertine.

OPPOSITE BOTTOM: In Gianni Angelli's office, the pallor of travertine and white lacquered window screens was further explored in the rich texture of the upholstered sofa and tufted lounge chairs.

OPPOSITE TOP: A "palace corridor" ran along the length of the perimeter wall for private access to the two Agnelli brothers' offices, conference room, boardroom, and, shown here, dining room. These rooms were separated by travertine panels set back from the perimeter wall.

OPPOSITE BOTTOM: The materials and colors of the space were chosen to complement the Agnelli art collection of classical, baroque, and modern sculptures and paintings.

BELOW: A copy of Canova's study of Pauline Borghese, the sister of Napoleon Bonaparte, rested in the long gallery next to an arrangement of Mies van der Rohe Barcelona chairs.

CONTINENTAL GRAIN COMPANY,
NEW YORK, NEW YORK, COMPLETED **1976**

DESIGN PARTNER: WHITSON OVERCASH
PROJECT MANAGER: H. S. FELDMAN

By the turn of the decade of the 1970s, the stock of towers constructed in the boom following the Second World War offered corporations the option of moving into an existing structure rather than building their own from the ground up. Thus began a process of renovating and retrofitting that has continued into the 1990s, transforming interior architecture into a highly marketable separate component of professional design services.

The new headquarters of the Continental Grain Company in an existing building on Manhattan's Park Avenue challenged SOM New York to create a corporate environment in a building that the firm had not designed. Davis Allen posed the question: "Why do we always have to use stainless steel? Gold doesn't necessarily have to mean that you are Louis XIV!" According to Raul de Armas, this thought activated "a change in our traditions, without changing the traditions themselves, moving from a cool vocabulary expressed in stainless steel to a warmer richness using bronze as the material of first choice."

The executive floors on the forty-eighth through fiftieth floors proclaimed this theme without equivocation, from the polished bronze of the interconnecting spiral stair of the reception gallery to its sisal-clad walls framed with bronze surrounds set against travertine flooring. The gleaming columns and doors that conferred luxurious distinction on the Agnelli suite now shimmered in polished bronze. The frame of the Brno chair was specified in bronze, and the marble-topped boardroom table was balanced on a blade of the same material. The chairman's office was furnished with his personal collection of museum-quality eighteenth-century French desk and side chairs, augmented by contemporary armchairs and sofa and a marble-topped conference table with a bronze columnar base.

Perimeter offices, conference rooms, the boardroom, and the dining room were enclosed behind partitions of bronze-tinted glass that afforded privacy in the interior yet sightlines to the main gallery. The gridded sunscreen first developed for the National Life project now became an important signature element in integrating "given" building standards with SOM's overall architectural concept.

Reflecting on the significance of this project in the evolution of the firm's interior design capability, de Armas said he considers Continental Grain "among the best work we have ever done."

OPPOSITE TOP: The executive floor was planned with nine offices, three conference rooms, boardroom, and executive dining room.

OPPOSITE BOTTOM: The Continental Grain project occasioned a further step in the evolution of the SOM style from High Modernism to a less strict adherance to the "less is more" doctrine. Thus, Allen's advocacy of exchanging cool white steel for a richer and warmer bronze represented an important turning point.

30'

ABOVE: SOM had designed many
beautiful staircases, but the sheer daring
of this sweep of bronze, swirling in a
spiral, gave special distinction to Allen's
increasingly respected reputation.

TOP LEFT: Bronze frames added a new dimension to the set of Brno chairs surrounding a marble-topped table supported on bronze columns in this conference room.

TOP RIGHT AND ABOVE: In the chairman's office, his personal collections of museum-quality eighteenth-century French antiques coexist harmoniously with modern classics and contemporary architectural detailing.

ALEXANDER & ALEXANDER,
NEW YORK, NEW YORK, COMPLETED **1978**

DESIGN PARTNER: MICHAEL MCCARTHY
PROJECT MANAGER: H. S. FELDMAN

This rehab of one floor of a 1960s tower on Manhattan's Avenue of the Americas for a major insurance company could be called a novel leap backward, incorporating references to the established aesthetic of interior architecture at SOM. For example, there was a reprise of elements from the Tour Fiat and Continental Grain projects. The executive offices were set back from the perimeter in a ''palace corridor'' and separated by freestanding partitions covered in coarse, handwoven linen and framed with polished bronze surrounds. The lacquered sunscreens first used in Nashville reappeared as an architectural statement. Bronze was used as a detailing accent on furniture: table bases, the bull-nosed edge of the bog oak boardroom table, and the trim of the glass-topped dining table. With a flash of inspiration, Allen detailed a wood-topped conference table with brass corners suggested to him by the finish of his Gucci wallet.

In place of a conventional art collection, Allen proposed a mélange of handmade folk art objects, assembling more than one hundred that he explained had been made for actual use in daily life in Africa, India, China, America, and other places. Among them were a Kashmir shawl, a Mennonite quilt, a red Burmese bowl, a red lacquer Thai teak bull, twin Yoruba figures, a collection of Pacific island ceremonial spears, an American eagle made in Scotland, and a model Chinese junk.

On the cusp of the 1980s and postmodern architecture, the project achieved a masterly balance between old and new, primitive and sophisticated. The traditional impression conveyed by the space was all the more remarkable because it was achieved within the constraints of a contemporary architectural aesthetic. Only a practiced eye and a secure taste could have combined Queen Anne chairs with a modern glass-topped dining table, placed a contemporary sofa on an antique oriental rug over a teak floor, or hung a quilt with the aplomb of a medieval tapestry as Allen did in this project.

ABOVE: **To complete the design concept of the Alexander & Alexander offices, Allen assembled a collection of more than 100 pieces of art, much of it in the folkloric tradition. The circa 1860–1865 American eagle seen on the axis of the ''palace corridor'' was carved from Northeastern pine and authenticated by laboratory analysis at Winterthur.**

30'

TOP: A "Palace Corridor" ran along the perimeter of the executive offices, repeating a theme of the Agnelli suite to considerable effect.

ABOVE: The Dayak wood carvings (foreground) displayed in the executive gallery originated in Borneo, while the remainder of the figures came from Mali, West Africa.

OPPOSITE TOP LEFT AND RIGHT: Weather vanes, antique quilts from Pennsylvania and Ohio, and a replica of a Chinese junk hand-carved in Canton were among the objects selected by Allen for display in the executive offices.

OPPOSITE BOTTOM: In the design of this small conference table, Allen was inspired by the bronze corners of his leather wallet to add finesse to an already elegant table. The "Lone Star Quilt" dates from 1890, and was sewn by Mennonites from eastern Pennsylvania.

RIGHT: The oak boardroom table top was embellished with a bronze bullnose rim. A saw-toothed Diamond quilt from Pennsylvania was hung on the wall.

BELOW: In the dining room, Allen had the courage to surround the modern glass-topped table with Queen Anne-style chairs, and to attach a mélange of ceremonial weapons from the South Pacific to the wall. The figures in the foreground are twin carvings from the Yoruba tribe of Nigeria.

JOINT BANKING CENTER,
SAFAT, KUWAIT, COMPLETED 1983

PARTNERS-IN-CHARGE: LEON MOED, WARREN MATHISON
DESIGN PARTNERS: ROY ALLEN, WHITSON OVERCASH

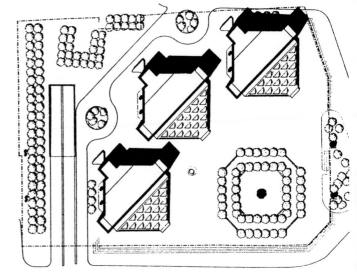

In the late 1970s, clients from the Middle East desirous of conveying an image of themselves as serious contenders in the world market offered U.S. architects exceptional opportunities to design on an unprecedented scale, largely unconstrained by budgetary considerations. Such a project was presented to SOM's New York office when three Kuwaiti banks (Bank of Kuwait and the Middle East, Industrial Bank of Kuwait, and Kuwait Real Estate Bank) elected to build their headquarters as a complex on a single site. Since the three eighteen-story towers were identical, the individual identities and separate functions of each business would be expressed exclusively through interior architecture and planning. The challenge to the design team was thus to create a different interior solution for each building while respecting the cohesion of the whole.

The solution was to plan each building to meet the differing functional needs of its owner, while using bronze and marble as unifying components elaborated by smoked glass, travertine, and wood. The clients wanted to be presented with a choice, so the Allen team developed six alternative schemes for the executive floors and twelve for the three banking halls, including sixteen "trays" of furniture. The bronze detailing that had its genesis in Allen's Continental Grain and Alexander & Alexander projects was accentuated here with complex surfaces of English burl oak and rosso Levanto and Paradiso marble.

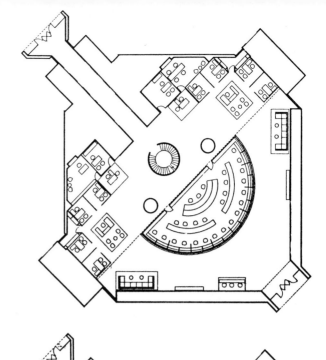

ABOVE AND OPPOSITE: A complex of three identical buildings on a single site comprised the headquarters for three Kuwaiti banks.

RIGHT: Although the exterior configurations were identical, the interior treatment of each banking hall reflected the individual character of each client. TOP: Bank of Kuwait and the Middle East. CENTER: The Industrial Bank of Kuwait. BOTTOM: Kuwait Real Estate Bank.

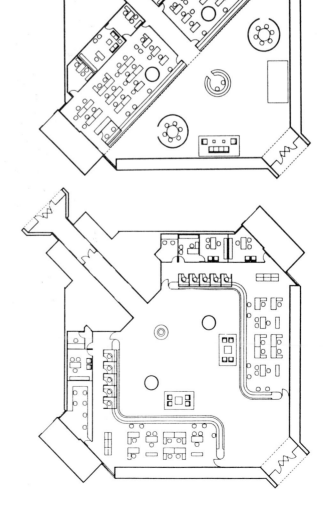

RIGHT, OPPOSITE TOP LEFT AND RIGHT:
The quality of the materials used in the
specially designed furniture for this
project reached the heights of luxury
appreciated by Middle Eastern clients.
Bronze, leather, lacquer, silk, English burl
oak, and ebony were called upon in the
design of desks, seating, and an almost
endless array of coffee and drum tables.

BELOW RIGHT: The "divaniere,"
enclosed within a bronze beaded curtain
framed in polished bronze under a ceiling
of the same material, suggests the
intimacy of an Arabian tent.

ABOVE: The abstract pattern of the
translucent screen of a reception area,
reminiscent of traditional Islamic
decorative motifs, was composed from
elements of the bank's logo.

NATIONAL COMMERCIAL BANK,
JIDDA, SAUDI ARABIA, COMPLETED **1982**

PARTNER-IN-CHARGE: GORDON WILDERMUTH
DESIGN PARTNER: GORDON BUNSHAFT

The design of this acclaimed tower in the historic city of Jidda, Saudi Arabia, began in 1977 and was virtually completed by 1979 when Gordon Bunshaft retired. Because of unforeseen difficulties with site acquisition, however, construction was delayed and the project not completed until four years later. As Bunshaft later reminisced to biographer Carol Herselle Krinsky, "They [the clients] wanted a great building. They wanted a unique building. They wanted a tall building." The twenty-seven-story triangular structure, built on a promontory overlooking the Red Sea, satisfied these criteria while also resolving the issue of merging centuries-old Islamic conventions and motifs with the modern requirements of international electronic banking.

The travertine-clad exterior presented a monolithic façade interrupted by three deep loggias punched into two elevations. These incisions represented the points at which the interior space was rotated and interlocked to form a secondary triangle. Air shafts, vented at the roof, were created in the resulting voids; natural light filtered into the interior floors through the tinted glass of the loggias. The ingenuity of the stacking plan readily explained the mystery and severity of the exterior.

Working with his friend Bunshaft for the last time in their thirty-year association, Davis Allen led the team of interior designers. The effort called upon all his world travels, long experience, and wide knowledge; his taste and appreciation of Middle Eastern culture; and his ability to understand concepts in their totality. As comprehensive as Chase and as open-ended as Mauna Kea, the project offered an opportunity that Allen recognized might never come again. He was, as ever, reluctant to claim personal responsibility. Nevertheless his deft eye and hand were clearly apparent in the delicacy of the meticulous detailing, in the opulence of the materials, never deteriorating into ostentation, and in the subtle layering of the SOM vocabulary with Islamic references.

Allen worked with furniture makers in Paris and Tours, presenting prototypes and mock-ups for client approval in Jidda as well as in New York. His familiarity with world markets enabled him to commission furniture in France, Italy, and the United States, carpets in Hong Kong, and woodwork in Germany. Bunshaft acknowledged Allen's contribution to decisions about the interior architecture, particularly in the selection of materials for the banking hall and executive floors, which included fifteen different marbles, one hundred types of upholstery fabrics, and more than twenty-five types of wood and veneers. More than seven hundred pieces of furniture and seventeen rugs were custom designed. Every executive office had its own unique carpet, wood and marble wall covering, and furniture, down to the last coffee table and wastebasket. Allen described the effect on the design team in a 1985 interview: "What happens when you have this unique opportunity is that the office becomes like a design studio. You are inspired. People blossom and become prolific. The whole team really got into the spirit of the thing; we could have gone on forever creating tables and rugs and everything we could think of."

National Commercial Bank marked the conclusion of Gordon Bunshaft's almost fifty-year career, proving that in his valediction he had not lost his ability "to draw strong forms and original conclusions," to quote Kevin Roche's tribute on the occasion of the award of the Pritzker Prize to Bunshaft in 1988. For Davis Allen, too, the project represented a sort of finale, and Roche's words could fittingly be applied to him as well. Two years later, at the age of sixty-nine, Allen was semiretired and had begun to take on the role of elder statesman, serving as a resource rather than participating in depth in each project. In 1990, as he entered his seventy-fifth year and his fortieth year with SOM, Davis Allen continued to inspire the firm that nurtured his talent and the generations of designers in the profession he has served with unassuming dedication. The interiors of the National Commercial Bank stand as a testament to his genius.

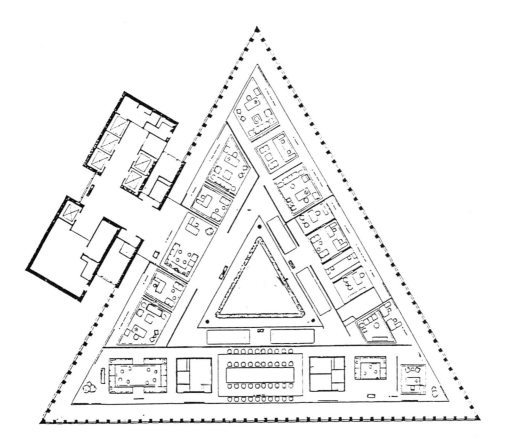

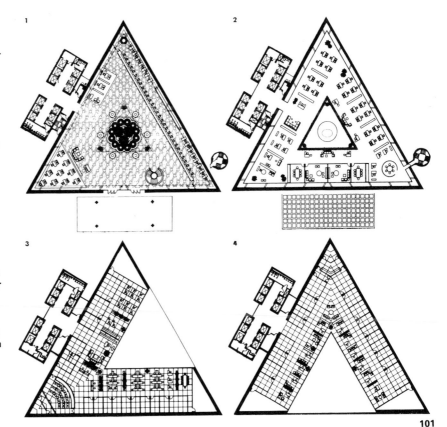

OPPOSITE: The twenty-seven-story tower is sited on a promontory overlooking the Red Sea. The triangular structure is juxtaposed with a six-story circular parking garage.

ABOVE: The executive floor in plan. The chairman's suite is at the base the triangle. An arcade, which references the traditional porch of residential architecture in Jidda, traversed the entire perimeter, capping the building with a notched frieze.

RIGHT: Four plan drawings illustrate how rotation of the triangular configuration of the building footprint at three levels resulted in the creation of loggias on two sides of the facade, and a central "void" vented through the roof for passive ventilation. 1. The banking hall, with a centered "oasis." 2. A mezzanine floor thirty feet above the hall was supported by three columns surrounding the "oasis." 3. The triangle was rotated on floors eight to seventeen to face the northeast. 4. Floors eighteen to twenty-seven resume the configuration of the building base.

LEFT AND RIGHT, OPPOSITE TOP LEFT AND RIGHT: Allen custom designed more than 700 pieces of furniture for this spectacular project, including a large variety of coffee tables in a number of shapes and materials, using lacquered wood, mirror-polished bronze, and clear and colored glass.

BELOW: The boardroom lounge on the executive floor was furnished with an oversized banquette set against the wall in the preferred Arabian manner. The rug was one of seventeen designed especially for the project.

ABOVE: The NCB Tower is considered by
many to be the last of the great modern
high-rises of the mid-twentieth century.
While the opulence of the interior
materials contrasts with the reserved
minimalism of the architecture, their
richness confirms that the change in
values posited by Allen in the Continental
Grain project was now firmly established
in the language of SOM's interior design.

PART THREE: THE LEGACY

In the years following the National Commercial Bank project, Allen remained involved in a continuing stream of projects. The Vista Hotel, nestled between the towers of the World Trade Center in downtown Manhattan, bore his signature in its resort ambience and the scale of the furniture in the public spaces. Allen's hand was also evident in the planning of the formal American Harvest Restaurant, which recreated the proportions of a New York town house in five spaces divided by vitrine partitions edged with polished brass. In a characteristic Allen touch, toys loaned by the American Museum of Folk Art were displayed within the vitrines. The Tall Ships Bar and Restaurant was inspired by the taverns of old New York, with images of square-rigged sailing ships etched on glass paneling; the polished brass detailing and wooden bar tops recall the finishes of the captain's quarters of a clipper ship.

ABOVE: The Tall Ships Bar in the Vista International Hotel, New York City. A high level of quality in materials and finishes was used to suggest the atmosphere of an old New York Tavern and the detailing found in a clipper ship captain's quarters.

OPPOSITE TOP: Presentation rendering of the Tall Ships Bar and Restaurant.

OPPOSITE BOTTOM: Presentation rendering of the American Harvest restaurant at the Vista Hotel. A New York town house ambience was created for the restaurant of the high-rise hotel at the World Trade Center.

OPPOSITE AND BELOW: As in many other projects, Allen's appreciation of native crafts was demonstrated in the display of early American dolls, figures, and craft objects within the brass-edged vitrine panels which divided the American Harvest space into five "rooms" of residential proportions.

RIGHT: A presentation panel of the materials employed in the Vista Hotel project, assembled for client approval, indicates Allen's thorough integration of sophisticated and naive elements within an interior environment.

Working with SOM partner Michael McCarthy, Allen contributed to four of the New York office's most visible projects of the 1980s: the Kuwait Chancery in Washington, D.C.; the Islamic Cultural Center of New York, which includes a mosque; Columbia Presbyterian Hospital; and the Al-Ahli Bank of Kuwait.

The chancery's eighteen-foot-high main reception hall is a decorative, vibrant space partitioned by teak screens embellished with bronze- and steel-filigree panels. "The combination of these metals was something outside the precepts of our heritage," McCarthy said.

> But Dave, referring to an Islamic scabbard, said 'It might be gold, but they might also have used some other metal such as silver.' That is what we did, but it had to be done in a very sophisticated and knowing way or it could have been vulgar. Working with Dave, you always had the feeling that you would pull it off. He has such tremendous courage. We worked so very closely on this project that I could never say where one started and the other took over. It was a true collaboration.

ABOVE: Consulting on the interior components of the Al-Ahli Bank of Kuwait, Allen participated in the selection of materials. Shown is the glass and metal screened dome constructed above the teller counter to provide for additional security for banking hall transactions.

OPPOSITE: In the dramatic main reception hall of the Kuwait Chancery in Washington, D.C., Allen's practiced hand was revealed in the decorative but always restrained use of a wide assortment materials, including bronze, steel, wood, marble, and granite.

LEFT: The teller counter at the Al-Ahli Bank was enclosed in a "bird cage" structure. The domed roof of the enclosure is shown in greater detail on page. 110.

BELOW: An elegant SOM-style staircase was executed with glass panels framed in polished stainless steel for the Al-Ahli Bank project.

Allen also advised on the Islamic Cultural Center project. "There isn't a color or a material that we haven't talked about. Everything passed in front of him," McCarthy said.

Speaking about the Columbia Presbyterian Hospital project, McCarthy revealed an aspect of Allen's professionalism that underlay his innate aesthetic sense.

> He consulted on the interior finishes and generic furniture, but there is a whole range of practical criteria on a hospital project, and Dave was the most practical person on the team. He always was. When we were faced with packing up materials for presentations on Middle East projects, it was Dave who devised trays that stacked together so that we could ship all that stuff in the most compact and safest way. He was always interested in all the aspects of process as well as in the final product.

As late as 1988, Allen participated in yet another large-scale project for a Kuwaiti client, the Al-Ahli Bank, once again calling upon his reserves of knowledge of Islamic symbols and references in order to consult on the interior architectural finishes and furniture. Of particular note was an array of coffee tables reminiscent of the National Commercial Bank project, designed using glass, bronze, and stainless steel in a variety of new patterns and shapes.

At SOM it had been and continues to be customary to develop original furniture designs based upon immediate proj-

ABOVE: Allen designed a range of
completely original coffee tables for the
Al-Ahli Bank. These pieces are
nevertheless reminiscent, in their variety
of shapes and materials, of the Jidda
project ten years earlier.

ect needs. From the vantage point of the 1990s, with its enormous market of available furniture, we tend to forget that until the 1970s the range of choice offered by manufacturers was extremely limited. SOM's philosophy of total design established criteria that related the scale, materials, and specific intended use of furniture to the overall architectural concept. These standards generally required unique solutions because the marketplace offered few compatible products. Thus, for the Inland Steel project in the mid-1950s, Davis Allen developed his "tin desk," which became the first

ABOVE: Allen's Andover chair was used to great advantage in the main dining room of the Palio restaurant designed by SOM, New York.

ABOVE: The Andover chair series, designed by Allen, was introduced by Stendig International in 1983 as a "new American classic." The armchair and side chair series features laminated beech frames and upholstered seats. Andover's generous scale and classic spindle construction make it appropriate for a variety of applications including conference, dining, and executive and residential interiors.

LEFT: Allen's intention was to create an "American" chair, related to the classic Windsor but with a contemporary feeling. The historic connotation is maintained in the spindle frame, while the laminated finish conveys a sense of up-to-date technology.

RIGHT: Working in collaboration with Carol Groh & Associates, Allen further developed his interest in the spindle vernaclular in a lightly scaled chair manufactured by Jack Lenor Larsen.

BELOW: Introduced in 1990, Allen's ladder-back Meeting House chair, manufactured by Hickory Business Furniture, was designed in association with Carol Groh's office. The maple-framed chair is intended for cross-over commercial/residential use, and is available in a variety of finishes.

modern desk made by Steelcase. He elaborated upon this design for the Chase Manhattan Bank headquarters later in that decade and further developed the concept in the late 1960s with his GF series, which was used in many SOM projects of the period. In his "gold" era, beginning with the Continental Grain project in the early 1970s, polished bronze took the place of polished steel; softer, rounded edges superceded the hard angles of high modernism in both tables and seating. This richer language, which reflected the prevailing taste for a more traditional corporate environment, was uniquely in tune with the preferences of Middle Eastern clients in the Jidda and Kuwait projects of the late 1970s and

RIGHT AND BELOW RIGHT: The Bridgehampton series for Stendig International consists of an armchair and side chair in two sizes (The Bridgehampton II model is an intermediate size), an armless cafe chair, and a high stool. The frame is beech, and the seat is available upholstered or in natural woven cane.

ABOVE: The Bridgehampton Café chair, installed in the bar of the Palio restaurant with a specially designed, accompanying table. The Café chair height is twenty-nine inches compared with the thirty-eight-inch height of its parent version.

1980s. The entire forty-year process of developing a consistent firm sensibility can be read within the time frame of Allen's career.

In his later years at SOM, Allen began to realize other ideas that had long simmered in his imagination. The result was furniture intended for generic use by the design community at large, appropriate for both the contract and residential markets. Best known is the Andover armchair and side chair series, manufactured by Stendig, which from its introduction in 1983 was recognized as classic design comparable to the Mies Brno or the Breuer Cesca chairs. Allen's Bridgehampton series, consisting of two armchairs, side chair, café chair, and high stool, also from Stendig, continued his exploration of the intrinsic Americanism of the wood chair that he had first expounded upon in his spindle chair of 1969. In 1988, Bernhardt introduced a line of casegoods that Allen designed in collaboration with Carol Groh & Associates. In a nod to postmodern conventions, this series expressed classical architectural themes in rich wood veneers with distinc-

ABOVE AND OPPOSITE: Since 1985, Allen has consulted with Carol Groh & Associates on a number of furniture design projects. The Brandon Casegoods collection, manufactured by Bernhardt, is a memorable example of their collaboration. Working with Groh partner Thomas Mahoney, Allen developed an extensive series of large-scale pieces with classical architectural motifs, including executive desks and credenzas; coffee and occasional tables; pedestals and cabinets; bookcases and computer work surfaces. Rich veneers are bordered with inlays of ebony and maple marquetry in the executive desk and executive credenza and storage cabinet.

BELOW AND OPPOSITE: The strong
architectural form of the Brandon
collection is demonstrated in three
components: table-desk (below),
credenza (opposite top), and the
executive desk (opposite bottom). Brass
drawer pulls may be specified in three
varieties including the Reed bar shown.

tive borders of ebony and maple marquetry. Also with Groh
& Associates, Allen designed an elegant, lightly scaled side
chair produced by Jack Lenor Larsen Inc. Allen's collaboration with Groh continued with the 1990 introduction of the
Meeting House chair from Hickory Business Furniture. Its
maple frame and ladder back recall the Shaker influence,
while the upholstered seat adds contemporary built-in comfort to its more austere reference point.

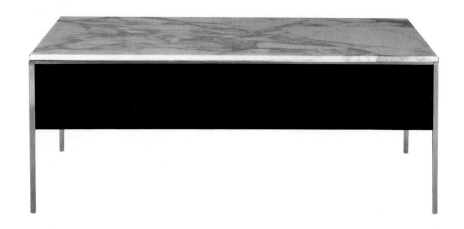

LEFT: The evolution from High Modern to transitional furniture design can be read in Allen's forty-year career. The desk he designed for the Chase Manhattan Bank in the late 1950s is a classic statement of the pared-down aesthetic of the period: marble work surface, black lacquer panels, polished stainless steel frame.

BELOW AND OPPOSITE: Thirty years later, with Carol Groh & Associates, Allen developed a transitional vocabulary in a furniture series slated for future production. The collection consists of executive desks, tables, seating, credenzas, and other storage components. The material is cherry wood with brass trimmings.

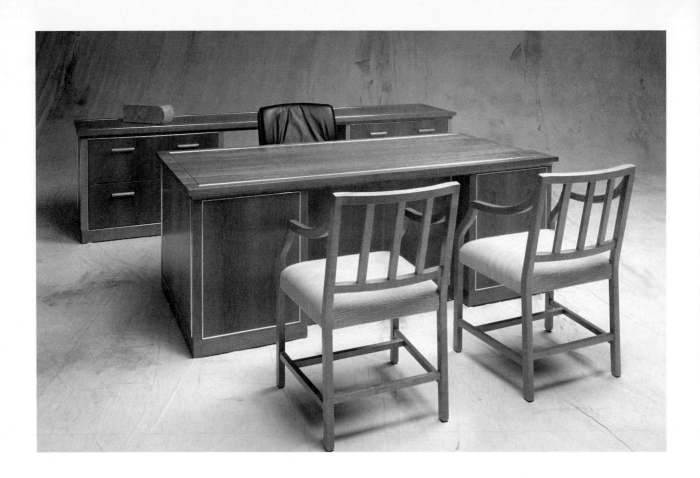

Davis Allen's legacy consists of dedication to high standards of professionalism allied with a warm regard for personal associations. Many long professional careers in retrospect inspire awe and admiration in many but affection in few. Davis Allen is an exception, having gained genuine love as well as respect from his colleagues of forty years. They recognize not only his abundant talent but his generosity in friendship. A consummate team player, Allen is quick to share credit for project responsibility, can teach without preaching, and is sensitive to the feelings even of people many years his junior.

SOM Design Partner Raul de Armas, responsible for the interiors of many New York office projects of the 1980s, recalled

> the way that Dave was always right. He
> carefully integrated everything in the project
> and created something that was part of our
> larger, standard way of doing things, always in

ABOVE AND OPPOSITE: Prototypes of the transitional series Allen designed with Carol Groh & Associates indicate his virtuosity as a form giver. The modified Victorian arm of the side chair and the use of lightly toned cherry wood with brass fittings on drawers and cabinet doors are in the vocabulary of the traditional. Yet the scale is completely in tune with contemporary tastes.

a new way, yet without offending those from whom the tradition had come or giving the sense that he was doing something hokey or fashionable. His is a particular talent that combines the strength of a concept and at the same time can be fully flexible about reworking it if there is a problem, while never abandoning the power of the original idea.

High in Michael McCarthy's estimation is that Allen

always developed two or three different schemes. If the owner liked the one that we liked least, it never fazed Dave; he just accepted it and went on. Other designers, less secure and less sure of their talent, would fight for their own ideas. The biggest lesson I learned from Dave is that there is more than one way of doing things: you have to have more than one trick up your sleeve. When you're hard-pressed and you've got to meet deadlines, and where you always want to have something new and fresh, it's invaluable to be able to think this way.

McCarthy studied architecture at Cornell and Harvard and joined SOM in 1964. He became involved with interior design for the first time during the American Can Company project, completed in 1970. "Interior design wasn't part of my architectural education, and I didn't know even how to begin," McCarthy said. "Dave was always very funny in his own quiet way. With gentle persuasion and a lot of humor he suggested that you could start with the horizontal surface, which could be carpet or wood or stone, and then you'd have a motif from which you might develop a scheme." Looking back on their association, McCarthy observed, "I always like Dave to look at the interior components of the work I'm involved in. I just feel better when he gives an opinion."

Those who moved on from Skidmore, Owings & Merrill to start their own firms or to become important members of other firms are no less appreciative. Charles Pfister, who spent sixteen years at SOM San Francisco before founding The Pfister Partnership in 1981, observed:

Dave had a great effect on all of us who were at SOM. Because he was so sensitive to scale and proportion and because of, for example, his use of beautiful precision-made objects against rough wood or rough stone, he imbued us with the same attitude. We absorbed it almost by osmosis because he taught by doing. His great thing was 'What if. . . . What do you think?'; that would start a whole dialogue going. He genuinely wanted to make it a team thing, which was tremendously good for your confidence, but more importantly it gave you a very strong idea that this was the way it was supposed to be done. I think that to this day people are amazed at the way we all still work, that we actually bring our young people along with us. Dave was the one who made that seem commonplace. And there's another unusual thing about Dave. He opened doors for me to many people—and he wanted to, which was very special.

OPPOSITE: The entry to the secretarial area (top) and a private lounge room (bottom), designed by The Pfister Partnership for Shell Central headquarters at The Hague, the Netherlands, exemplify Charles Pfister's belief that Allen's influence remains strong in "beautiful precision-made objects" used in conjunction with richly textured materials sensitively tuned to the scale and proportion of a space and its furnishings.

In agreement was Margo Grant, whose distinguished reputation was honed in her eleven years at SOM before joining Gensler and Associates in 1973.

I think that part of the teacher instinct in Dave is to get you to participate. And I've tried to do that with my people at Gensler. When I first worked with Dave on Mauna Kea I was quite inexperienced; probably the best thing that could have happened to me at that stage of my life was that Dave opened so many doors to me professionally and personally. For example, when we were working on Mauna Kea, Dave included me in Laurance Rockefeller's invitation to lunch at the Rainbow Room. I'd never met anyone like a Rockefeller and I was scared to death. And his habit of asking 'What do you think?'—and actually meaning it. He was never afraid to let you know that your opinion mattered.

LEFT: For a petroleum company in Houston, Gensler and Associates designed an Allen-influenced, transitional space that included an eclectic mix of materials, textures, and decorative elements, including antique and contemporary furniture combined with folk art objects and warm wood flooring laid in a diagonal pattern.

BELOW AND OPPOSITE BOTTOM: Executive offices for a major Manhattan financial institution were designed by the New York office of Gensler and Associates. Managing Principal Margo Grant acknowledges the lessons she absorbed from Allen in the comfortable "clubby" ambience created in The Commons, an executive lounge complete with a working fireplace (opposite) and a private staircase (below) linking the space with the executive floor below.

Carol Groh, founding partner in 1979 of the highly successful New York–based Carol Groh & Associates, first met Allen when she joined SOM Chicago in 1967:

I was really excited when he would come into the office, because he was the guru of the best design available. I think that Don Powell, Bob Kleinschmidt, and Ursula Damien, all young [SOM] designers at the time, felt the same way: there was this tremendous respect for him. My generation used to die to have Dave work with us. We wanted to learn and there was so much to learn from him. He did so much for my self-confidence; I'd never have been able to do what I've done so quickly in my career if Dave hadn't been my mentor. He felt it was important to have young people participate in client meetings, even if the client was Lyndon Johnson, Aristotle Onassis, or Gianni Agnelli. I try to do that now with our own young people in the firm. It's a whole different world from the drawing board: it's selling, it's presentation, it's psychology, and even if they don't say a word, it's experience.

I've learned so much, too, from Dave's wonderful way of designing with objects and incorporating them into the space. When you talk about a creative person, Dave has such a talent and can take from what he sees and experiences. He has the ability to retain what he has seen and put things together so that new ideas and new directions evolve. It's not that those ideas just pop into his head. He has a unique ability to pull from the past, from all of his experiences, and from all of that put new things together. I honestly try to achieve that, because no one is just creative out of the blue. It's got to come from some relationship, and that is what Dave is superbly good at.

ABOVE AND OPPOSITE: Carol Groh recognizes the Allen legacy in the Union Trust Bank (Signet) headquarters, Baltimore, Maryland, designed by her firm. In the chairman's dining area (above), rich wood paneling is contrasted with soft beige wool carpeting. Allen's Andover chairs are placed around ebonized mahogany tables. A custom-designed desk presides over the reception area of the executive floor (opposite top). The drama of the banking hall (opposite bottom) is emphasized by the use of four different granites and back-painted glass teller counters, with "a pull to the past" in the decorative floor pattern.

Chief among the characteristics that distinguish Davis Allen, as those with whom he has worked reaffirm, is his capacity for forming lasting friendships. Since his personal life and his work were seamlessly knit together, these associations became enormously important to his professional success. His lifelong habit of observation was cultivated in world travels undertaken during projects; the resulting friendships evolved into a worldwide network of invaluable resources. As he remarked, "If you ask questions and tell people what you're doing, they are usually very helpful. So, I was always able to travel fast and not stumble around too much." A self-confessed good shopper, his instant perception of intrinsic worth was extraordinary. Margo Grant remembered "shopping" for the Mauna Kea project. "No matter if it was a Cost-Plus in San Francisco, an antique shop, a hotel gift shop, or a department store, if there was only one good thing Dave would walk right to it. He would almost be drawn to it because of his knowledge and his taste."

"Show me your best . . . (hotel, club, restaurant, house, garden)" was an inquiry that brought impressive dividends. On Mauna Kea or in Dallas, in South Africa where he toured Swaziland and Lesotho to understand local conditions and traditions before starting work on a hotel complex in Johannesburg, or while journeying through Uganda, Tanzania, and Kenya to study national parks for a possible Rockresort undertaking, Allen's research led him to ingenious solutions respecting indigenous cultures, colors, and artifacts.

All these experiences contributed to the lifetime achievements of Davis Allen, a legacy of rare value in terms of both the work itself and the manner in which it was performed. In a rare moment of self-evaluation devoid of understatement, Allen allowed that "these things probably amount to quite a compendium of work and experiences." Then, adding a surprising coda, he went on, "That is if you combine it all with my earlier time of working on the farm, working on the ranch, working in the screw factory."

To a perhaps naive question about the educational value of the farm, the ranch, and the screw factory to a career in interior architecture, Allen responded almost reprovingly, "It taught me about life. Life, that's all. That's where you learn that it doesn't matter if it costs fifty thousand dollars or fifty dollars or five dollars.

Ultimately, the legacy of Davis Allen devolves from this profoundly simple declaration:

"Life, that's all."

Project List

In the years from 1950 to 1990, the name Davis Allen appeared as Senior Interior Designer on more than fifty projects designed in the New York, Chicago, and San Francisco offices of Skidmore, Owings & Merrill. In many of the projects listed here, Allen was involved in the preliminary design concept and mock-up stages or as a consultant on furniture, color, or art. Credit for the final resolution, he believes, belongs to others. The major projects for which he does accept credit, while demurring at the claim of total responsibility, are described in Part Two: The Projects, 1950–1990. Davis Allen, a paradigm of team participation, consistently recognized the architects, engineers, interior designers, and indeed the clients who made possible the integration of disciplines into the group practice that is the fundamental principle of SOM's philosophy.

Manufacturers Hanover Trust Bank, Fifth Avenue Branch, New York, New York
Completed 1954

Istanbul Hilton Hotel, Istanbul, Turkey
Completed 1955

Ford Motor Company, Dearborn, Michigan
Completed 1957

Avon Products, Inc., Morton Grove, Illinois
Completed 1957

Reynolds Metals Company, Richmond, Virginia
Completed 1958

Inland Steel Company, Chicago, Illinois
Completed 1958

General Mills Inc., Golden Valley, Minnesota
Completed 1959

Crown Zellerbach, San Francisco, California
Completed 1959

First National City Bank, New York, New York
Completed 1959

Union Carbide Corporation, New York, New York
Completed 1961

Chase Manhattan Bank, New York, New York
Corporate Headquarters, completed 1961
410 Park Avenue Branch, completed 1959

Albright-Knox Art Gallery, Buffalo, New York
Completed 1962

Businessmen's Assurance Company of America, Kansas City, Missouri
Completed 1963

IBM Corporation, Armonk, New York
Completed 1964

Mauna Kea Beach Hotel, Kamuela, Hawaii
Completed 1965

Marine Midland Bank, New York, New York
Completed 1967

Texas Bank and Trust Company, Dallas, Texas
Completed 1969

National Life and Accident Company, Nashville, Tennessee
Completed 1970

American Can Company, Greenwich, Connecticut
Completed 1970

Lyndon Baines Johnson Library, Austin, Texas
Completed 1971

Carlton Center, Johannesburg, South Africa
Completed 1972

Philip Morris USA Cigarette Manufacturing Plant,
Richmond, Virginia
Completed 1974

Marine Midland Center, Buffalo, New York
Completed 1974

Joseph H. Hirshhorn Museum, Washington, D.C.
Completed 1974

General Electric Company, Fairfield, Connecticut
Completed 1975

New World Center, Hong Kong
Completed 1975

Agnelli Suite, Tour Fiat, La Defense, Paris
Completed 1975

Olympic Tower, New York, New York
Completed 1976

Victory Carriers, New York, New York
Completed 1976

Continental Grain Company, New York, New York
Completed 1976

Texaco Inc., Harrison, New York
Completed 1978

Alexander & Alexander, New York, New York
Completed 1978

Washington Post, Washington, D.C.
Completed 1979

Hyatt International Hotel, Kuwait City, Kuwait
Completed 1979

Vista International Hotel, New York, New York
Completed 1981

King Abd al-Aziz International Airport, Jidda, Saudi Arabia
Completed 1981

Commercial Bank of Kuwait, Safat, Kuwait
Completed 1981

Joint Banking Center, Safat, Kuwait
Completed 1983

National Commercial Bank, Jidda, Saudi Arabia
Completed 1982

Kuwait Chancery, Washington, D.C.
Completed 1982

Georgia-Pacific, Atlanta, Georgia
Completed 1982

Manufacturers Hanover Trust Corporation,
New York, New York
Completed 1983

Irving Trust Company, New York, New York
Completed 1983

Al-Ahli Bank of Kuwait, Safat, Kuwait
Completed 1988

Merrill Lynch & Company, New York, New York
Completed 1988